THE TEENAGE WRITER

THE TEENAGE WRITER

A Guide to Writing for School and Creativity

TIMOTHY HORAN

ROWMAN & LITTLEFIELD
Lanham • Boulder • New York • London

Published by Rowman & Littlefield
An imprint of The Rowman & Littlefield Publishing Group, Inc.
4501 Forbes Boulevard, Suite 200, Lanham, Maryland 20706
www.rowman.com

86-90 Paul Street, London EC2A 4NE, United Kingdom

British Library Cataloguing in Publication Information Available

Library of Congress Cataloging-in-Publication Data
Names: Horan, Timothy, author.
Title: The teenage writer : a guide to writing for school and creativity / Timothy Horan.
Description: Lanham, Maryland : Rowman & Littlefield, [2023] | Includes
  bibliographical references and index. | Summary: "Writing well is very important in
  order for teenagers to be successful in high school and college. Beyond school, many
  teens write to be creative or to express themselves. This book is an accessible guide to
  help teens improve all aspects of their writing skills, from writing a research paper to
  writing for fun"— Provided by publisher.
Identifiers: LCCN 2023001354 (print) | LCCN 2023001355 (ebook) | ISBN
  9781538153178 (paperback) | ISBN 9781538153185 (epub)
Subjects: LCSH: English language—Composition and exercises—Study and teaching
  (Secondary) | Composition (Language arts)—Study and teaching (Secondary)
Classification: LCC LB1631 .H7195 2023 (print) | LCC LB1631 (ebook) | DDC
  808/.0420712—dc23/eng/20230426
LC record available at https://lccn.loc.gov/2023001354
LC ebook record available at https://lccn.loc.gov/2023001355

To Michelle.

You have always been my favorite song.

Contents

Acknowledgments

Every book I write is the glorious result of the people and schools who nurtured my childhood dreams, and who whispered to me—sometimes silently, and sometimes in eyes that looked like poetry—*"you can do it."* And now, I want to thank all of them . . . because I *remember*. I remember all of you—and I will never forget you. First, eternal thanks to my parents, who gave me the best advice I ever received: "Go to college." To St. John's University (in Queens, NY), especially their wonderful English Department. You made me *read, and read, and read*—and *write, and write, and write*. It was beautiful, and has become one of the centerpieces of my life. Deep appreciation to Long Island University, who gently propelled me into a marvelous teaching career. Profound thanks and appreciation to the wonderful people at Rowman & Littlefield, for the kindness and professionalism they have shown me over the years.

Tremendous gratitude to my good friend Jeremy for helping me when I needed it, and infinite appreciation to the teenagers who contributed to this book . . . just because I asked them to: Annabelle, Birgitta, Elizabeth, Emily, Jack, Jenny, Meghan. *You are all amazing.* Love and gratefulness to dearest friends Tycho and Oscar (now departed), for giving me two lifetimes of love and loyalty. Wild adoration and unending gratitude to beautiful Michelle—

ACKNOWLEDGMENTS

For our dances in the dawn—
In the sunrise of the spring—
In the whisper of the wind—
On the surface of the sea.

INTRODUCTION

HOW TO BUILD A BIRDHOUSE

I'm thrilled that you decided to spend this time with me. I enjoyed writing this book very much, and it is my utmost desire that you enjoy reading it and learning from it. This makes sense, because we read for only two reasons: we read for *enjoyment*, and we read to *learn*. And now, since we're going to be spending some time together, I want to tell you a little about me, and how I got here.

When I was five years old, I knew I would be a writer. It was very cool learning my destiny that early in my life. Honestly, I had no choice in the matter; it was like discovering the color of my eyes (they're blue, if you're curious). So, while I was still in kindergarten, becoming an author emerged as the shining dream of my life, and books became the glittering treasures of my heart. Books were just "my thing"; I don't know how else to explain it. As I got older, the dream of being a writer never left me, and I feel very lucky, because there is no gift I'd rather have (and I absolutely mean that). So, I fell in love with books and reading and writing quite early, and it has been a lifelong romance.

As a young child, I read all the time, and wrote tiny "books" by folding blank paper in half. I would write a title, provide my name as author, and draw a picture representing the action of the plot. Inside the two folded halves I would write the story, usually some outlandish adventure set in a broiling jungle. On the back cover I would write a summary of the story. For me, it was a form of *playing*. Of course, English quickly became my favorite subject. I loved walking into my English classes, and I loved the books we read. All the reading I had done helped me to understand books and stories, and writing came easily to me. In high school I was spotted as having "talent," and I was placed in an English class called "Talented and Gifted" (TAG English). I adored it, and did well with it, and got As on all my writing. It was fun.

Looking back, however, I now realize that something priceless was missing. Through all my years of writing in grades one through twelve—and receiving good marks on my essays—*I was never taught how to write.* Teachers *assigned* writing, but they didn't *teach* students how to write. Wait—I want to slow down for a moment, and emphasize this important point: teachers *assigned* writing, but they didn't actually *teach* it. And this situation persists to this day in our schools.

I was lucky. I managed to write well without receiving any true writing instruction. How? I learned from reading a great deal and my desire to be a writer, mingled with some natural aptitude. I enjoyed the assignments, wrote from my heart, and imitated my favorite authors. But still, I didn't really know how to write, and I was about to learn a very painful lesson. When I got to college, the dean looked at my high school transcript, and said, "Oh, you were in TAG?" and quickly placed me in a class called "Advanced Composition."

I'm sure he meant well, but I'm not sure he did me a favor. I walked into that class feeling good about myself and about life, but about to learn a painful lesson: college bore little resemblance to high school. The work was more rigorous, the standards were higher, and the environment demanded greater independence. About a week into the course, we received our first assignment, which was to analyze Jonathan Swift's brilliant satire, "A Modest Proposal." (Please read this when you're twenty-one years old. It's the greatest satire in the English language.)

I composed my essay quickly and joyfully (after all, I was on my home turf), and handed it in. I did a good job on it—or so I thought. Imagine my shock and horror when (a few days later) the professor read it aloud to the class, discussing its weaknesses in a rather blunt and merciless manner. He was quite thorough, and he didn't hurry, either. I blushed and sweated, and nearly fainted when I saw "D+" written in red ink next to my name (accompanied by red notes scribbled all over my essay). I was embarrassed and horrified, whispering to myself that a *D+ is just above an F!* I was a good writer, and I felt my dream of becoming an author fading into a wounded whisper of something sad and sorrowful. That's a true story. *What happened?*

Looking back, I now see that, like my earlier teachers, this professor *assigned* writing, and *graded* it, but didn't actually *teach* it. This was an "advanced" college course, and the professor just assumed that students had been taught how to write. Here is the reality of the eighteen-year-old me: My writing was good, but I didn't know how to write a focused and organized academic paper. I didn't understand the structure and model of scholastic writing, and I certainly wasn't ready to write for college. I was expected to have mastered something that I had *never been taught*, and the intellectual fog was so dense that *I didn't know that I didn't know* it. (I also struggled with math, but that's another story for another day.)

So why am I telling you all this? Because I want you to know that I've been there. I know what it's like to struggle with writing, and I know how you're feeling. To all my readers who are students (you're probably in high school, or middle school, or college, but students of *all* ages are welcome here), I want you to know this: *you are not alone.* When a teacher gives you a writing assignment, you receive it with a sense of dread, because you don't know what to do. *You don't know what to do.*

You have never truly been taught how to write for school. You don't understand the writing assignment or its purpose, and this thing becomes an unpleasant and mysterious *chore* that must be endured and suffered through. You don't know how to start or how to proceed with a composition, so you procrastinate and leave it to the night before it's due. Then you sit down in a mild panic and write because you have to hand in *something*, and *something* is better than *nothing*, and you hope for a C or a D, because a C or a D is better than an F. I get it.

And what did you learn from that experience? You learn that writing is a difficult and mysterious task that holds no rewards except handing something in so you don't have to think about it anymore. You rejoice that this thing is finished, but you don't feel a sense of pride in the composition you produced (and I *want* you to feel a sense of pride—in your writing, and in yourself). You develop a dislike of writing, and you don't know how to fix this situation.

Yes, I understand all of that (because I've been there), and I know how difficult and lonely it is. And I want to say something else: *this is not your fault.* How can you do something you were never taught to do? I also want to repeat that *you are not alone.* Nearly all the students I have worked with (from high school up through college, and sometimes even graduate school—and there have been *thousands* of them) simply do not know how to write.

For the great majority of students of *all* ages (including the ones in all your classes), the writing process is a frightening mystery. I also want to say this: *don't lose hope.* You are reading this book, which means you have taken your first step toward learning how to write. Stick with it—and stick with *me*—because *you can do it.* I will show you how. And now, I want to pause for a moment, and explain something to you.

Please don't take any of this as criticism of your teachers. It's *not.* In fact, I want to *compliment* all the teachers out there, because they are doing wonderful work. I've been a teacher of high school English, and I consider it one of the toughest jobs in the world of education. It is more intense and demanding than you can imagine. For me, teaching high school English was like having two full-time jobs. There is the prep and the teaching, and there is the unending parade of papers and exams to read and grade at home. It is an unbelievably difficult and time-consuming profession, and teachers often feel as if they "don't have a life."

I get it. I see the problem from both sides of the teacher's desk. But still, there is a problem that young writers must confront, and here it is: *most high school students simply don't write well.* It's a big problem, and we need to fix it. Got any ideas? I sure do. In my previous book (*Writing and Growing: Transforming High School Students into Writers*), I argue for the creation of high school writing courses given to *every* student in the nation, in *every* year in high school. Until that happens, I—and my books—will teach you how to write. And this brings me to a pair of important questions about a pair of siblings named *audience* and *purpose*:

Who is the *audience* for this book?

What is the *purpose* of this book?

The primary audience for this book is *you*. I wrote this book for young people (especially teenagers) who are having a hard time writing for school. I also wrote it for young people who want to improve their writing skills in general—maybe for college and career. I also wrote it for young people who—like me—dream the impossible dream of becoming a writer. (And yes, my friends, dreams really do come true. And, when that happens, it is a joy beyond belief. So, cling to your dreams, and nurture them until they come true.)

I also wrote this book for anyone who wants to understand the writing process. However, if you're a teacher, or an adult who is somehow involved in the education process (or who just wants to learn how to write), this book is for you also, and it will give you great insights into teaching (and learning) the writing process.

And this brings me to the *purpose* of this book. It's really very simple. The purpose of this book is to *teach you how to write*. I deeply understand the writing process—in fact, there is nothing I don't know about writing. Throughout my life, I have immersed myself deeply (and happily) inside the world of writing, and there I found great beauty and profound simplicity. Good writing is beautiful, and *great* writing is *art*. And yes, I have known (and helped) high school students who became excellent writers, so *you can do it*. I promise you. Learning this wonderful art form is very doable, and I want *you* to do it. And you *can* do it.

At its heart, writing is a very simple process. And now, I want to give you a rule, and I want you to remember it:

The best writing is clear and simple.
The best writing is clear and simple.
The best writing is clear and simple.

Wait, let me explain what I just did. In this book, when I say something *three times* (like I did above), that means it's *very important*, and I want you to *memorize it*. (I do this several times in this book, and I always use it for *emphasis*. I also use it because it's effective, unique, and it's *cool*.) Many of the things we have been taught about writing were *wrong*, and need to be unlearned. Good writing is already inside you, so part of the process of learning to write involves *unlearning* layers of bad stuff until the real *you* emerges on the page. And that's always a great thing when it happens.

And here, I want to pause for a moment and talk about the *writer's voice* I'm using here, in this book. I want you to understand that the writing in this book is very good (and please excuse the compliment I just gave myself, but it's true). As a writer, I always strive to make my writing *clear and simple*, and to have a slightly poetic and musical feel to it. Can you see it? Can you hear it? Can you feel it? Look for it and find it, because it's there.

As I developed the voice for this book, I focused on my primary audience: *teenagers*. I wanted to write a book that teens would enjoy, and that sounds a bit "conversational" in nature, sort of like we're chatting on a spring morning before class begins. I wrote this book for *you*, I kept it clear and simple, and I really hope you like it. And now, I'm telling you, keep your own writing *clear and simple*. So, ditch the thesaurus, and stop trying to write like a kooky college professor. You're not a kooky college professor, so stop trying to sound like one. You're a young person, and the world is opening up to you, and that's a beautiful thing.

When you write, I want you to write from your heart. When you write, I want you to sound like *you*. I want you to develop your own individual writing style that sounds like nobody else in the world. When a piece of writing becomes a *mirror* in which you see yourself—when you read your own writing and you find *yourself* there—you're on your way to becoming a *real writer*. But how will you do this?

That's what this book is for. I will tell you how; I will pass all of that knowledge along to you. After that, *you* will put in the time and the practice. You will do your homework, complete your essays, and watch your writing improve (and, we hope, watch your grades improve also). This growth and this change don't happen overnight, but I promise you it will happen if you work at it and don't give up. If you stick with me and my methods, you will grow into an accomplished writer.

As I wrote this book, I consulted a small group of high school students, and I asked them about their experiences writing for (and in) high school. You will meet these students in the following pages. I use their first names only, and I promise you they are real people, and their responses are honest and genuine. Our correspondence was through email, and I asked them all three simple questions:

What do you find difficult about writing in high school?

How did you *cope* with the difficulties of writing in high school?

How did you grow as a writer, and what successes did you achieve?

So, as you read this book, you will encounter original writing from actual high school students. I will provide their responses, and I will discuss the things they said. This will be helpful, because many of *you* (my readers) are having experiences similar to these students. Finally, I will use these students' responses, difficulties, and observations to provide you with ways to grow as a writer, despite the difficulties you are experiencing. There are always ways to triumph over obstacles. *Always.*

Besides discussing the experiences of real students, I will also discuss my own experiences as a teacher and writer and human being. To do this, I will tell stories. I like telling stories, and I'm good at it. And all of my stories contain a lesson or two. Remember, we're all in the business of *learning*. And, while we're learning, we want to be interested and have some fun. So, as you read this book, be on the lookout for stories, and be on the lookout for lessons at the end of my stories. As always, I'll do my best to make my stories—and the moral of the story—engaging to read.

As I composed this book, one of my main goals was to make it fun and interesting. As I wrote, I kept asking myself this question: *Would someone take this book to the beach and read it?* That was my litmus test as I wrote, and I think I succeeded. This was very important to me, because we all learn more when we're engaged and interested. And now I will tell you two stories that both have lessons at the end.

When I was studying for my doctorate in English, a professor at the university started a writing center, and he chose *me* to be its first assistant director. I was thrilled and flattered, and *so* excited to start this new chapter in my life. While working in the writing center, I tutored college students all the time, teaching them the gentle art of *writing*. As I did this, I learned something very quickly. Most of these college students *could not write*, and here's how I found out.

During these tutorials, the students would always bring me a paper they were writing. After they handed me the paper (so I could read it), I would ask them a question: "What's this paper about?" Amazingly, many of them thought for a moment, looked puzzled, and said, "I don't know." Imagine that. These were bright college students. They were writing a paper for a course they were taking, and *they didn't know what the paper was about*. Here's another story.

In a few years, you'll go to college yourself, and then you'll graduate. If you continue your studies to get a master's degree or a doctorate, you will be a "graduate" student (and I hope you do this; it's an amazing experience). Well, a long time ago, I took a graduate course in education, and I got to know the professor very well (I will call her Dr. Levine, but this is not her real name). We would chat before class or after class, and on several occasions, she confided her frustrations to me. And this was Dr. Levine's biggest complaint: "These are *graduate* students, and they can't write!" When they wrote a paper and handed it in to be graded, the writing was poor.

Think about it. These were all college graduates (most were in their late twenties), and they were going for master's degrees in the field of education. They were going to be *teachers*, and they could not write! One evening after class, Dr. Levine told me that she was teaching students who were getting *doctorates* in education. When you pursue a doctorate, the last thing to do before graduating is to write a book-length project called a *dissertation*. It's sort of like writing an essay for class, except that this essay needs lots of research, and is three hundred pages long.

Well, Dr. Levine told me that she was helping doctoral students write their dissertations, and then she said something that shocked me: "They are writing their *dissertations*, and they *can't write!*" It was an amazing thing to hear. They were going to be *teachers* with the title of "Doctor," and *they could not write*. So, what's the moral of these two stories? It's very simple: Don't be so hard on yourself—you're not the only one who struggles with the writing process. You are not alone.

And now, I want to give you an analogy. At the end of my analogy, I will reveal some of the secrets of writing. An analogy is when you talk about one thing, and you compare that thing to something else. *"Subject A is like subject B."* For example, here is a quick analogy. *Earning my doctorate was like running a marathon that's a thousand miles long.* That's an analogy. Well, here's another analogy: *Learning to write is like learning to be a carpenter.* A carpenter is someone who builds things out of wood. A good (or great) carpenter builds *beautiful* things out of wood that will last for centuries. I'm a very good carpenter, and I love building things.

Okay. So—

I live in a lakeside log cabin. I built a library in my cabin, and it holds my two thousand books. I did a beautiful job on it, and it was another lifelong dream come true. I've always wanted a library in my house, and now I have one. It took me months to complete, and it's my favorite room. I love books, I love being creative, and I love libraries, so you can imagine how this project made me feel. I also built a desk in that room, and that's where I sit and read and write my books. I'm in my library right now, sitting at the desk I built and writing this book. I'm happy to be here and doing this, and it's a very special place to be, and makes me very happy.

Anyway, writing is like carpentry. Wait, let me say that again: *Writing is like carpentry.* Pay attention, because this is important. When you're a carpenter, you start with basic materials (tools and wood), and you create something new that has never existed before. It's an act of *creativity*, and at the end of it, something new exists that didn't exist before. It's a marvelous reward to stand back and feel proud of the thing you built, and say to yourself, *I made that.* Keep my analogy in mind; *writing is like carpentry.* And now, I want to use this analogy to teach you a few things about writing, and I want you to really understand what I'm saying.

Imagine *me* on a summer morning in my backyard, getting ready to build something. Beautiful day, sunshine and birdsong, icy lemonade, and I'm enjoying the gift of summer and sunshine and being alive on planet Earth on this beautiful morning like it's the glorious dawn of creation. I take my tools and lumber out of my shed, and I set them up and organize them so I can use them. And then I stand back and look at everything, and whisper to myself, "I don't know what to build."

That's an analogy for a fledgling writer who has been given an assignment to write something, but thinks, "I don't know what to write." It will *never* happen with me in writing *or* carpentry. *Never, never, never.* When I set up my tools and lumber, *I always know exactly what I'm going to build.* I have thought about my project a thousand times, made sketches with measurements (you might call these sketches *outlines* and *rough drafts*), and I understand my project down to the millimeter.

The same is true with my *writing.* When I sit down to write, *I always know what I'm going to write about* on that particular day. *Always, always, always.* I always know the subject I'm going to write about. I *never* sit down to write wondering what I'm going to write, and what will appear on the screen. *Never, never, never. I always know what I'm going to write about,* and I also set a goal for myself.

For example, my goal for a certain day of writing might be this: *Write three pages about writing, and use the carpentry analogy you've been thinking about.* Yes, this carpentry analogy has been brewing in my mind for over a year, and I was waiting for the right time to use it. Well, the right time is *now,* and in the introduction to this important book I'm writing. And here's the lesson I want you to remember: Whenever you sit down to write, you should always *know what you will write about. Always, always, always,* and every single time. I know that sent a chill pulsing through you, but don't worry. I will show you how to do this, I promise. And it will be easier than you think.

And now, time for another carpentry analogy. When I set out my tools and lumber in my yard, I never stand there and "wait for inspiration." *Never, never, never.* Inspiration doesn't show up when you need it or when you ask for it. *It doesn't happen.* And now, let me give you the secret of avoiding "writer's block." Do you know what *writer's block* is? It's a common complaint among writers (even great ones), and it refers to times when you sit down to write, and you just can't think of anything to say. You stare at the screen (or the blank page) for a long time, in a sad sort of frustration, and then you get up and get something to eat, and maybe turn on the TV. You *want* to write, you really do, but the words don't show up. The words just won't flow.

A few years ago, I read something very insightful about writer's block. There was a famous (and brilliant) Irish writer named Oscar Wilde who lived a long time ago. When someone asked him if he ever experienced writer's block, he said this: "Plumbers don't get plumber's block, and doctors don't get doctor's block; why should writers be the only profession that gives a special name to the difficulty of working, and then expects sympathy for it?" ("Writer's Toolbox," 2022). It's a terrific response to the question, and it makes an excellent point.

Writing is difficult. *Do it anyway.* When's the last time you heard a landscaper say, "I'm sorry; I can't cut your lawn today. I just don't have the inspiration to do it"? Writing can be difficult sometimes, but *sit down and do it anyway.* Write your ideas down, even if they don't sound good. You can make them sound pretty later. I never get "carpenter's block." I always know exactly what I'm going to build, and then I go and build it. It's the same with writing. I never get writer's block. *Never, never, never.* I always know exactly what I'm going to write, and then I sit down and write it.

Time for another carpentry analogy. Picture it: our tools and lumber are waiting for us in the sunshine and birdsong of beautiful early summer. Let's say I'm teaching a young person how to be a carpenter. This student (let's call her Michelle) knows nothing about carpentry, and she shows up in the morning well rested and excited to learn (and hands me an extra-large coffee, thank you very much).

If I'm an *ineffective* carpentry teacher, here's what I can do: I can point to my tools and lumber, and say this: "Your assignment is to build a birdhouse. Do a good job on it, and build a good birdhouse, because I will be grading it. Good luck." And then I walk away and drink my coffee, leaving Michelle to figure things out on her own. That would make me a bad carpentry teacher, wouldn't it. *I gave Michelle an assignment, but didn't teach her how to do it.* Sound familiar?

And you know what Michelle will do? She will stand there alone, staring at the tools and lumber, wondering what to do, and feeling sad and demoralized. It's a terrible place to be. Finally, she will give up, and walk away from my yard (and from *me*), and gently shut the garden gate. She will feel like a failure, and she will believe it's her fault that she can't build a birdhouse. And she will learn to hate carpentry. Well, it's *not* her fault. She was never taught the basics of carpentry. I *told* her to build a birdhouse. I didn't *teach* her how to build one. See what I mean?

Let's talk about my analogy. I gave Michelle an assignment (*build a birdhouse*), but *I didn't teach her how to do it*. Isn't that what's happening in school? Teachers give you assignments, but they don't truly teach you *how to write*. And now, I'll describe how I would *really* teach this student the basics of carpentry. When Michelle shows up, I greet her with a smile, thank her for the coffee, and show her my tools and lumber. I tell her we're going to build a birdhouse *together*. I show her the sketches I made, I talk about them, and I talk about birdhouses. And now Michelle understands the project, and she understands the *goal* she needs to accomplish.

I discuss my tools and my lumber in greater detail, and I talk about each one, and what it does. And maybe I show her how to use my compound miter saw to cut wood at perfect ninety-degree angles, and maybe I show her how to drill pilot holes in pine so that the pine we're using (a softwood) doesn't split along the grain when we countersink the galvanized Phillips-head screws. But I explain all of this in great simplicity. I teach Michelle all of these things, and I help her practice these basic and newly learned skills. And she learns. And I teach her, and I teach her, *and I teach her.* And she learns, and she learns, *and she learns.*

And now, let's get practical. How should you use this book? Here's what I want you to do: First, read this book carefully. Read it with a *pencil* in your hand, and write all over it. Flag important passages that speak to your heart; write question marks where you don't understand something; write *"Aha!"* or *"Yes!"* when you have gained a surprising insight into some aspect of the writing process. Writing these notes is called *annotating,* and you should do it in every book that you read. (Except for library books. You don't own those, so use "sticky notes" instead.)

And now, I want to pass along something I learned while serving as an officer in the United States Marine Corps. When things got very difficult (and things were almost *always* difficult), the instructors said this: "If you're not having fun, you're doing something wrong." That's a rule that I treasure and still hold close to my heart. And now, to this day, whenever I feel a little down, or a little tired, or a little discouraged, I repeat it to myself: *If you're not having fun, you're doing something wrong.* It makes me stop and think, and it makes me wonder: *What am I doing wrong? What could I be doing better? Am I approaching this with a positive and healthy attitude?*

I'm not trying to sound "preachy" here; I'm really not. But I'm *alive,* and you're *alive,* so why not make the best of it and approach our lives with a positive attitude? Why not find the smiles that lay deep in our hidden hearts? That's what I try to do, on a daily basis. I love to have fun, and I want you to enjoy the experience of being alive on planet Earth, because it really is a wonderful thing.

The more I teach, the more convinced I become that my main job is to *help students fall in love with the experience of being alive.* So please enjoy this book, because I wrote it to give *you* the priceless gifts of learning *and* pleasure. If you are reading these words right now, you are my audience and you are my student. So, I urge you to enjoy the process of learning to write, and watching your magnificent mind blossom. And remember this: in all of the universe, there is only one *you.* Like it or not (and I hope you *like* it), that makes you very special. You are truly one of a kind. And that's a fact, not an opinion.

And this leads to my next question—and maybe yours too. *How will you learn to write?* Your journey starts by reading this book and absorbing the principles contained here. I know what I'm talking about, and in these pages, I will explain the writing process in terms that are very human and understandable. As you read this book, you will find a writing system that I developed through years of studying, teaching, tutoring, and writing. The writing system I created is simple, effective, and designed for teenage minds. It is also, I believe, the most effective writing system in existence for teaching young people how to write, and for preparing them for college-level writing.

If you read this book carefully (and I suggest reading it at least *five times*, because *repetition* is where deep and long-term learning occurs), you will emerge with a solid understanding of writing as an act of authentic creativity, and you will develop and possess the priceless and lifelong gift of *writing.* It is a gift that you will use over and over, long after you have left the classroom. And now, before we move on, I want to say two more things:

You don't know how to write? You are not alone.

And one other thing: all of that is about to change.

Teens Talk

What Is Difficult about Writing for School?

OUR TEENS ANSWER QUESTION 1

As I wrote this book, I asked a group of current high school students to tell me how they feel about writing. I wanted to understand their connection to writing, and I wanted to learn about the parts of writing they find most challenging. To do this, I asked them *three questions*, all through email. I encouraged them to be honest in their answers, and they were. And why did I do this? Simple. I wanted to find out how current high school students feel about writing, and I wanted to understand the things they find most difficult. Listening to their concerns was very interesting, and I am going to share all of it with you.

In this chapter, I provide their responses to the first question: *What do you find difficult about writing in high school?* As you read their responses, I'm certain that you will recognize and understand the things they find most challenging. I'm also confident that you will identify with their struggles and see yourself in the things they said. Their responses were quite illuminating (and often consistent), and helped to pinpoint the struggles of contemporary teen writers so that I can discuss them in this book.

Below, you will find the students' responses. After each response, I provide a summary of their *challenges*, interpret them slightly, and offer a broad overview of how they can be remedied. In the second half of this chapter, I provide writing instruction that focuses on their major concerns, and the things they (and you) need to learn. Please read it carefully. In that portion, you will begin your journey toward learning to write. Here are the students' responses.

STUDENT RESPONSES
Annabelle (Eleventh Grade)

Whenever I write, I always try to have fun with it. Writing isn't one of those topics that I dread or love, it really depends on its purpose. For example, when it is about a topic or genre that I like, I enjoy it greatly. But when I'm assigned a specific topic, sometimes it is really hard to follow and it frustrates me. When I first receive a writing assignment, I tend to skim over the assignment, then read into it deeply. What I find to be most difficult is that most of the time I overthink the prompt or get completely off subject when planning and/or writing. If the prompt is a subject that I do not enjoy, then I don't enjoy the writing.

Also, most of the time I'm concerned about the grade that I may receive. Will my teacher disagree with my point of view? Am I writing enough? Am I writing the right thing? Etc. Writing assignments usually overwhelm me and I rush to get them done. I feel as though when this happens, there really is no purpose to the assignment, because it overwhelms me and I don't take the time to absorb the information and learn it. For me, writing my own way (but utilizing the skills that my teacher wants me to develop) would help me enjoy writing and learning at the same time.

When I sit down to write for a high school assignment, I struggle with many things. Whenever I'm given a word limit, I tend to write double (accidentally). I just start to ramble on, trying to get my point across in an ineffective manner. Secondly, I struggle with time management. Large writing assignments cause me to write too much in one sitting, causing me to ramble and make mistakes. Also, I get into a zone, where I fail to learn the skills that the assignment is trying to get me to learn and/or get off track. Assignments with due dates stress me out and cause me to make more mistakes than usual.

Depending on the assignment, I always second-guess myself when finishing it, since it is going for a grade. I rarely feel proud of the work I accomplish, and get nervous when I'm stalking the grade book for a grade. For any writing assignment, I always wonder if I could've done better, what comments my teacher is going to say, what mistakes I made, etc. I love to write pretty much any type of assignment, but I have great difficulty when those assignments are dictated by a rubric or outline.

One final difficulty I find when it comes to writing in high school is the writing process and certain aspects. Certain English teachers that I've had in the past have had different rules than others. For example, one teacher will have a writing suggestion while another teacher completely disagrees with that rule. I feel like certain writing strategies are in the "eye of the beholder," or in this case, the teacher. As for aspects, I always struggle with beginnings and endings of paragraphs and papers in general. I never know how to start or end a thought; I end up just rambling on until I feel as though I'm through.

I love writing deeply, but when the creative factor has been dictated or taken from me, I have difficulties and don't enjoy the assignment.

My Reaction to Annabelle's Response

When Annabelle receives an assignment that doesn't interest her, she finds it difficult to write. She also tends to overthink the prompt, and sometimes wanders from the topic as she plans and writes. She is uneasy about the grade she might receive, her teacher's potential reactions to her project, and to the quality of her own writing. She tends to write *double* the amount she needs, and sometimes "rambles." She has trouble with time management, and due dates make her nervous. She has difficulties with the rigid structures of certain assignments and finds it difficult when new teachers appear to "contradict" things she had learned from former teachers. She also struggles with beginnings and endings of paragraphs, and with writing assignments in general.

All of these are common complaints among students, and they can be fixed. Annabelle needs to clearly understand the writing task, and then stay focused on it. She needs to overcome procrastination and become more organized. As she learns how to write, she will grow confident in her writing and in herself, and the unease that surrounds her writing will begin to fade and vanish. Her anxiety about writing will *decrease* as her knowledge about writing *increases*. She will begin to approach "uninteresting" writing assignments as simply another form of homework and another task to complete, and her interest in these writing assignments will grow. In this book, I address all of Annabelle's concerns.

Birgitta (Eleventh Grade)

In general, I like writing. I like it because it helps to organize your ideas and articulate them to others. When I get a writing assignment, I feel a bit of dread or excitement, depending on what the topic is.

When I actually start writing, the hardest thing is writing a strong start and ending that aren't overly repetitive. When I do finish, I feel proud if I wrote something that I feel has substance. Sometimes I feel as though I could have tried better. I usually feel like this after writing an academic essay. I like to write fiction, but have no original ideas. Academic essays feel like they always have the same topics.

One thing that I think is mysterious about writing is how some people churn out essays back-to-back without tiring.

My Reaction to Birgitta's Response

Birgitta likes writing in general, but dislikes writing assignments that focus on "uninteresting" topics. She has difficulty writing introductions and conclusions and tends to make them repetitive. She is occasionally proud of her work. She likes to write fiction, and would like to write short stories, but she has trouble generating original ideas. She craves more variety in her writing assignments, and does not understand how some writers can write consistently (and successfully) without becoming exhausted.

When Birgitta understands more deeply the structure of academic writing (especially the *purposes* of introductions and conclusions, and the differences between them), her writing will improve and feel more natural to her. When she understands the simple structure of *stories* (discussed in chapter 6 of this book), she will have an easier time generating ideas for short stories (or any kind of fiction she wants to write). As she learns more about writing (and grows as a writer), her "uninteresting" assignments will feel friendlier, and she will be able to write consistently without feeling overwhelmed or exhausted.

Elizabeth (Eleventh Grade)

I love writing. As a child, I was constantly reading, and as I got older, I started hankering for a creative outlet. Since my art skills leave much to be desired, I stuck to what I knew and started writing. I love taking a blank page and making something that speaks to the reader. Writing and writing assignments are pure possibility.

That said, when I'm writing, my biggest struggle is usually following the rules. If given an assignment to write specifically about one topic I have a habit of going slightly off track and bringing other topics in. I'm also very harsh on myself. Sometimes every word has to be perfect, and I have in some cases spent more time than is necessary editing, or editing so harshly that I erase all that was unique in the piece. I'm definitely still learning to edit well while retaining a signature style. However, I rarely find myself completely unhappy with what I've written. There's always at least a sentence or two that I'm proud of, even if I go completely crazy with my edits.

My Reaction to Elizabeth's Response

Elizabeth enjoys writing. However, she needs to understand her scholastic writing assignments more clearly, and she needs to more deeply comprehend the thing she's writing about. She tends to wander in her discussions and is extremely hard on herself. She wants to make her assignments "perfect" and overedits her writing, removing her individual writer's voice from what she has written.

Elizabeth needs to understand her writing assignments in crystal simplicity, and her writing must stay focused on the topic of her paper. She needs to remain highly organized as she prepares to write, and she must make sure that her *writing* is focused and organized as well. When it comes to editing, Elizabeth needs to learn what "works," and what doesn't. This comes with time and practice. She must also stop being so perfectionistic in her writing. This is a common trait of *all* writers, even the best professionals. In the world of writing, there is an old saying that I find very helpful: *a paper is never truly finished; it is merely handed in.*

Emily (Eleventh Grade)

Writing is an extensive and integral part of our English classes each year of high school. There are many different levels of preparation that students possess as they enter high school regarding the process and techniques of writing. To be honest, I do not always feel very confident about writing because every teacher has a different approach. When I sit down after being given an assignment, I normally formulate a plan in my head and compartmentalize my thoughts. I find this especially helpful to make it more manageable for myself and make the process less stressful.

However, when it comes time to transcribe my thoughts onto paper, I find it difficult and a bit overwhelming. I struggle with constructing my ideas into a complete piece of writing. I do feel proud once I complete a writing assignment because I know that I really did put a lot of effort into it. A persuasive or argumentative style of writing is more challenging for me than something such as a personal narrative because I feel that there is a lot of gray area about the correct way to incorporate a counterclaim. It can be tricky to bring up the opponent's side while still supporting your claim.

Each year, it takes me a little time to adjust to a new English teacher due to their different teaching styles. Some teachers may even contradict others' methods, which may be confusing as a student. I feel that there is a lot of leeway with regard to how people express themselves through writing, and what makes a great author truly great. The rules of grammar can be confusing at times because of the many guidelines that people interpret differently. The fact that there is so much open to interpretation leads me to believe that the English language is one of our greatest mysteries.

My Reaction to Emily's Response

Emily finds it a bit confusing that different English teachers have their own unique methods for teaching English. For example, the writing methods taught by Emily's eleventh-grade teacher appear to "contradict" what she learned last year from her tenth-grade English teacher. Emily also has a difficult time expressing her ideas clearly and transcribing them onto paper. She finds argumentative essays especially challenging and has a difficult time writing her counterarguments (which she calls "counterclaims").

As Emily grows as a writer (and practices the techniques contained in this book), she will begin to understand that writing, at its heart, is a very simple activity. She will begin to accept teachers presenting material differently, and she will learn from *all* of them. She will also be able to more easily (and fluently) transfer her ideas onto paper or onto the computer screen. Through writing additional argumentative essays, she will more deeply understand their purpose and structure, including the challenging section of counterarguments. I discuss all these topics later in this book, and I explain them quite clearly.

Jack (Twelfth Grade)

I've been writing for a long time, and I usually enjoy doing it. I took creative writing this year, and I really liked it. Being given creative prompts in my senior year was helpful, and is one reason why creative writing is one of my favorite classes. I'm not always in the mood to write, nor am I always inspired, but writing always remains important to me as a craft.

During my first three years of high school, I felt that all writing had been focused on nothing but "finishing the assignment," as opposed to writing something I was proud of. Receiving assignments like that were part of what made writing for school so hard. Some teachers didn't teach much about how to write a paper, only the format and the subject. They would give us a general subject to write about, but I would like specific things to write about. On occasion they'd give an example of a previous student who wrote the same kind of essay, but generally they expected for you to know everything already.

I also have problems with organization. When I write, I feel like my ideas aren't really organized. I also have trouble coming up with my own original ideas. When I do research, I feel like I'm just writing down things that others have said, like I'm writing the same paper they did. I also have trouble blending research with my own writing. I don't really know how to insert a source or a quote into a paper I'm writing.

The hardest part about writing in high school is the fact that the work is sort of dry. I didn't do research papers on stuff I cared about, I followed strict guidelines, and the subjects were never something I was interested in. I know the difference, because in my senior year I was given a choice to write about something that I was passionate about, as opposed to a topic I selected from a list. I also found that this paper was the easiest for me to write, as well as the most enjoyable.

The hardest thing about writing for me is actually gathering the motivation to do it. Once my pen is on the paper it's always a lot easier to get things done. I'm especially bad with writing pieces that require citations, like research papers. But I really like writing fiction.

My Reaction to Jack's Response

Jack enjoys creative writing. However, when it comes to his scholastic assignments, he finds it difficult to get motivated. He feels he hasn't had enough writing instruction and would like to receive more guidance for his writing projects. He wants his writing to be more organized, and he desires to generate more original writing in his projects. When he performs research, he is not sure how to incorporate quotations into his writing, and he's not sure how to analyze research and comment on it. He is also unsure how to cite quotes properly.

When Jack learns (and understands) the basics of writing academic papers, his motivation to write will increase. He will accept "uninteresting" assignments more readily, his writing will become more organized, and it will contain more original thought. He will learn how to explain and comment on the research he includes in his writing, and will be able to properly (and easily) cite all research and have it relate to an accurate bibliography. I discuss all of this later in this book, and I present it clearly, so that my readers can learn it and practice it.

Jenny (Tenth Grade)

I wish creativity was more encouraged in writing, as it would improve engagement and the students would receive the same benefit. I always advocate for the inclusion of creative writing in the English curriculum. While we analyze fiction, we don't get to write it ourselves. Most students would be much more interested in writing if they could convey their themes and ideas in a way unique to them.

What is most difficult to me when it comes to writing is using a formal tone rather than letting my style leak into impartial essays. I also tend to write too much. I struggle to be brief and concise in my reasoning and ensure everything relates to the theme of the text. One of the best parts of writing is learning the rules, so that we can innovate and break free from them. We are taught to eliminate all personal stylization and stick to a brief, structured response. While I know this is necessary, it is exhausting when we cannot learn to express ourselves.

Another thing I struggle with is a sense of organization. As I mentioned above, we are taught a specific format and style to use, and if we diverge from it, our work is not accepted. I tend to be more creative and struggle to find a healthy balance between dry organized structure and deeper, overly personalized analysis.

When it comes to writing, I also tend to struggle with procrastination as it relates to a lack of motivation. I often dread certain writing assignments because of the rigid format we have to follow. So I push it off to the last moment and rewrite many drafts and finally settle on something that just feels average.

Lastly, I struggle to write clearly. I have difficulty briefly getting my point across. I have an idea but have trouble translating it to paper.

My Reaction to Jenny's Response
Jenny craves creativity in her writing. When it comes to scholastic assignments, she "dreads" them and procrastinates. She has trouble writing in a formal tone and struggles to make her writing more organized. She also tends to write too much and has difficulty expressing her ideas clearly.

When Jenny more deeply understands the purposes and structures of academic writing, she will approach these "uninteresting" assignments with more motivation. This will help her to overcome procrastination. As she develops as a writer (and learns the basics of scholastic writing), her writing will become more organized, and she will find it much easier to write in a formal academic voice.

When she understands writing assignments in their *simplicity* (truly a breakthrough in a writer's development), her writing will become more focused and more *muscular* (she will use fewer words to write higher quality papers). With practice (and through using the methods I describe in this book), Jenny will have a much easier time expressing her thoughts clearly.

Meghan (Twelfth Grade)

When I write in school, many times I have gone off topic to speak and write about what truly matters to me (or even what's just on my mind) rather than the objective given. I've felt so deprived of creative writing that I found myself doing this in other classes as well, like history. I'd take any chance to turn the question around and do something creative with it. I think the good writers in high school nurture their writing skills, whether it be writing on their own time or reading.

What I find difficult to write the most are conclusions. I don't want to repeat everything I said, and I don't want to make it too simple, "and that's why I think that." My go-to option is to end with a rhetorical question, but I have a hard time closing the essay without it. I know how to use transitioning words and such, and I'm not super familiar with what the content in the conclusion should look like.

Often when I'm in English class, I'll be among the first to finish an assignment and there will be a long, awkward period where no one wants to be the first person to turn it in. So we all wait a while, which sounds silly, but in the moment, I think a lot of us worry we missed part of the assignment or we were rushing.

My Reaction to Meghan's Response

Meghan craves more creativity in her scholastic writing and has difficulty when given assignments that don't interest her. When she writes academic papers, she attempts to "tailor" the topic to her own interests and do something creative with it. This can often generate distinctive original writing propelled by creative inspiration. However, it is also a risky approach, and may result in a paper that does not address the requirements of the project (which may result in a lower grade). Meghan also has trouble writing conclusions.

When Meghan becomes more fluent in the principles and purposes of academic writing (all contained in this book), she will understand her writing prompts (and the goals of the assignment) in a much greater simplicity. This will allow her to stay focused on the topic and will reveal opportunities (and methods) to include *creativity* in her academic writing. She will accept "uninteresting" projects more readily and will understand the purpose of conclusions and how they are constructed.

WRITING LESSONS
It's Time to Stop Procrastinating

Many writers (including professional writers) struggle with procrastination. And what is procrastination? Procrastination means you put things off until later, or until the last possible moment—and sometimes later than that. When it comes to writing, this is very common among fledgling writers. Why do young writers tend to procrastinate? For one thing, it's because writing is hard work, and involves lots of concentration. But it's also very rewarding.

However, the major reason that young writers procrastinate is because *they don't really know what to do*. They don't truly understand the task they've been given, and this lowers their motivation. How can you do something when you don't know how to do it? When you understand the assignment and the writing process—when *you know what to do*—writing becomes a much friendlier activity, and you'll want to tackle it sooner rather than later. And you'll feel better about it—and better about *yourself.*

This is one of the reasons I'm writing this book. I want you to understand writing thoroughly. *I want you to know how to do it.* I want to dispel all the mystery, so that writing becomes a familiar activity, like putting your shoes on in the morning. When you understand writing deeply, you'll know exactly what to do. You'll be more inclined to start it early, rather than leaving it to the night before it's due. Or not handing it in at all. Being late with an assignment, or not handing it in, causes tremendous stress in your life, and you don't need that. That unwritten paper will keep you awake at night, and it's an awful place to be.

When you get a writing project, here's what I want you to do. First, make sure you *understand the task.* Read the assignment description five times, and learn exactly what you need to do. *What kind of paper is it? What is it asking me to do? When is it due? How long does it have to be? Does it require research? How many sources should I include? Do I need a bibliography?* Understand the thing *in its simplicity.* Here is your test for understanding what you have to write: *Can you explain the project, in simple terms, in one sentence, to family or friends, and have them understand it?* If you can't, then you don't really understand the task.

If you're even slightly unsure about the assignment, or about what kind of paper to write, *ask your teacher what you need to do.* Always *be polite and respectful.* Your teacher will appreciate this, and see you as a student who is interested, and who wants to do well. This will impress your teacher, and she will be "on your side" and anxious to help you. And this is always a good thing.

As you're learning the task of the assignment, take notes and make notes about the project, and don't lose the notes. You'll depend on them later. You can't perform a task well if you don't understand what you need to do. *Understand the doggone project.* Know what you have to do. This is the first step to overcoming procrastination and writing a good paper.

When you get a writing assignment, *start it right away*. Start it that day, or the day after (at the latest). Don't wait longer than that, or else it gets *cold*, and is pushed into the basement of your mind where it festers in darkness behind a closed door covered in cobwebs. It moves to the back of the line, and other things get in front of it. Start by getting organized with regard to the project. Make a list of the tasks you need to accomplish, and write them down in order.

Do a little work on the project *each day*, for perhaps one hour (and an hour will *fly* by). One hour a day for five days will feel like nothing. Five hours straight the night before it's due will feel like an eternity. And it won't be your best work (probably quite the opposite). I suggest working on the project for at least *ten days*, for perhaps one hour each day. *Get it done*, and you will feel amazing. All your friends will be complaining about having to do it, while your project will be complete. And probably be a very good paper.

As you plan your paper and begin writing, make sure you set goals for each day. If you want to get *really* organized, make a schedule for yourself. Write down your goals for each day, and then *meet them*. Your schedule might look like this:

Monday: Do my research, and find three articles for my paper.

Tuesday: Read the articles, and highlight three useful quotes in each article.

Wednesday: Make a detailed outline.

Thursday: Start writing my first draft, and write one full page.

Friday: Continue my first draft, and write a second full page.

If you make a schedule like this, and stick to it, you can't fail. As you grow as a writer, you'll get better at knowing what you have to do, and in what order. Your writing assignments will start to feel familiar (*hey, I got this*), and the writing schedules you create will be easier and more helpful. When I'm writing a book (which is pretty much all the time), I always set a goal for the day, and then I meet my goal, *no matter what*.

When I wrote my first book, I learned very quickly (and by accident) that a thousand words equals *three pages*. It just seemed perfect for me, so my usual goal is to write a thousand words a day. (Think about it: a thousand words a day for one month equals nearly a hundred pages of writing. That's an accomplishment for *anyone*, and a month goes by very quickly.) To write my three pages a day, I get up at three o'clock in the morning and I write for two hours before work. Every single day. But that's me.

If I don't meet my goal, I write again when I get home from work (and it's difficult then, because I'm tired). Is it a difficult schedule? Yes, it's difficult, but it's also deeply rewarding. And it's also kind of fun. I'm doing something special, while the rest of the world is sleeping. And it's much better than the stress of *not writing* when I need to be writing. That would literally keep me awake at night. And it's much better to be awake *writing*, than awake *worrying*.

Please understand that my system works well for me, but it's very extreme, so don't do it. Find another way to do your own writing, and always try to get eight hours of sleep each night. And remember: next time you want to procrastinate, just put it off until later.

Learn From *All* Your Teachers
Several students above said that their "new" English teachers present material differently from their *former* English teachers. This

"contradicts" what students learned previously and can be a bit confusing. I get it. It's a fact, and it simply cannot be changed. We all see the world differently, and, because writing and literature are both art forms, we are all going to have differing (subjective) views on them. However, this is a *good* thing, and I'll tell you why.

When educators teach you differently (as they *should*), it presents an excellent learning opportunity, and will expand your mind and your education. I wouldn't have it any other way, and I want you to take full advantage of it. To do this, I want you to approach all your classes and your teachers with an open mind, and be prepared to learn from them, no matter how unique their voices are.

In my years of teaching, I have seen this over and over. For example, while chatting with other teachers, I learn how they approach individual works of literature, and how they teach them to students. And they always differ from my own methods. Rather than argue with them that *"I'm right and you're wrong,"* I try to understand their differing viewpoints, and it has enriched my teaching a great deal. I'm constantly borrowing ideas from other educators; it's like receiving a precious gift.

For example, while one teacher may teach Shakespeare's *Macbeth* as a story of *ambition*, another will teach it as a story of *fate*. And who is right? In this case, they both are. *Macbeth* is a story of ambition *and* fate, so there is good learning to be had from both teachers (and both themes). Reading the play through these differing lenses will help you to understand the play (and the characters) better, and will help you to understand the complexity of the world. Things are rarely as simple as they seem.

As a teacher, I have sometimes encountered resistance from my students. Occasionally, a student will raise a hand, and say, "Mrs. Smith taught us this differently last year." Essentially, the student is saying, "I learned something different, so you are wrong." I'm *not* wrong, but that's not the point. One of the best things about education is hearing ideas from differing points of view, and I always explain this to my students.

If teachers taught the same material every year, all the same, that would be a problem. It would also be boring and repetitive to hear the same thing over and over. Do you really want to hear the same material, presented in the same way, year after year? Or do you want to build upon your knowledge, expanding it with differing viewpoints?

So, when teachers present the same material in different terms, listen to them and learn from them. Add it to your increasing store of knowledge. You'll like some points of view more than others, and you'll understand some concepts more than others. All of this is healthy and contributes to your education. So please— listen to what *all* your teachers have to say, and embrace this as a wonderful learning opportunity. Because that's what it is.

GET CREATIVE IN YOUR THINKING—*AND* YOUR WRITING

The students' concerns described above are fairly common among high school writers, and among young writers in general. However, I want to start by discussing their overwhelming desire for *creativity* in writing, because many students and readers can identify with this. In one of my previous books (*Let's Create Writers: Writing Assignments for Grades Seven and Eight*), I polled about a hundred middle school students regarding the types of writing assignments they enjoy most.

After crunching all the data, here are the top three types of writing that middle school students crave (presented in order, from page 177 of my book):

1. *Creative writing assignments*

2. *Writing about themselves*

3. *Writing about things that interest them*

This was not terribly surprising, and it carries over into high school as well. In my years teaching high school students, I find that their feelings on the subject don't differ greatly from their junior high counterparts.

Several of our students above thrive on creative assignments and enjoy writing about things that interest them. When I was a teacher of high school English, I tried to give each of my classes one creative writing assignment each year. It might be to write a short story, or it might be to write themselves into the book we just read, or something like that. I always tried to make it challenging and fun. When the class wrapped up in June, most of the students said it was their favorite assignment of the year, and I always liked hearing that. When I was in high school, I would have loved an assignment like that.

However (and I'm sorry to say this), there's no easy way to "fix the system," and I'll tell you why. Teachers have very little choice in what they teach. They have a curriculum to follow, and there is very little wiggle-room in the curriculum to teach other things. Teachers don't have a choice in the matter; they *must* follow the curriculum, and that's just a fact. I was able to give my students a fun project because I went through the curriculum at a fairly rapid pace, and this left room for a creative assignment.

The other reason that teachers teach "academic" writing assignments is to prepare students for college (and I really want you to understand this). When you get to college, virtually all your writing assignments will be academic in nature (unless you take a class in creative writing). For example, in college you will be required to write papers such as *informative essays, analytical essays,* and *academic arguments.* Essays like these are always challenging to write, and the standards in college are higher than in high school, so you must be prepared to write scholastic papers on a higher level. There's just no way around this, and if teachers didn't prepare you for college, they would be doing you a disservice. I really want you to understand that. But don't lose hope; there are still ways you can express your creativity.

Teachers don't have much freedom in *what* they teach, but they do have some freedom in *how* they teach, and this is where you might find your creativity. For example, you can *politely* ask your teacher this: "Will we be doing any creative writing in this class? Because I really love that sort of thing." And then listen to what the teacher says, but please don't argue with your teachers. You can *speak* with teachers politely and respectfully, but *don't argue with them.* That never turns out well, and is always the wrong thing to do.

If the teacher says you won't be doing any creative writing over the year, you could say this (if you're an ambitious sort): "I understand. But if I wrote a short story, would you be willing to look at it?" Here, the teacher might give you an enthusiastic "Sure, I'd love to!" or the teacher might say, "I'm sorry, but I'm just too busy for that." In either case, accept the teacher's verdict, thank the teacher for listening, and then politely end the conversation. The teacher might get back to you a few days later, and say, "I've been thinking about what you said . . ." This has happened to me more than once.

And there's something else you can do to satisfy your hunger for creativity. Now, pay close attention. You can approach your writing assignments with a creative spirit, and try to make them interesting to you and the reader. If you're bored while writing something, I guarantee the reader will be bored also (and that's something you want to avoid). I'm very good at this, and it's not possible for me to have a "boring" writing assignment. If I were given one, I would immediately think, "How can I make this interesting? How can I make this fun for me and the reader?"

A few years ago, a student told me that she was given an assignment in middle school that she enjoyed. It was to write an essay answering this question: "How Do You Eat an Ice Cream Cone?" It's a cute question, but sort of meaningless. After thinking about it, I decided to challenge myself. *If I received that assignment, how could I make it different from other students? How could I make it more interesting, and make it meaningful? How could I have fun with it?* And I decided to write a short story that somehow—*somewhere*—contained an ice cream cone.

My story was about a boy named Danny (and Danny is *me*) who had a summer job working in an ice cream parlor. It's a Saturday night, and it's very quiet, and Danny is bored and lonely. And then a girl walks in. She was about his age, and he had seen her before. She was short with dark hair, and a little chunky, and she wore a haunted expression on her face and in her eyes as if life had already hurt her, as if she was lonely and afraid to be hurt again. But she was cute, Danny thought, and her eyes were green and pretty.

She was wearing just a little too much makeup and had put on a little too much perfume. But still, she was dressed nicely and she smelled good, like a field of flowers in the early summer. But she didn't order anything. She seemed nervous (Danny saw that her hands were shaking), and she left quickly without saying anything, and without buying an ice-cream cone. As she walked out, Danny noticed that her pretty green eyes were glassy and shining, and her hands were trembling as she pushed the door.

As Danny stood there in the silence of Saturday night, he suddenly realized that she was there to talk to *him*. She liked him, but she was too shy to speak. With great sadness, Danny realized that he missed a wonderful opportunity. He missed his chance to talk to her, and maybe to go out with her, and maybe even to fall in love. He was deeply sorrowful, and hoped he'd see her again. And that's where my story ended. Of course, the title of my short story was, "How to Eat an Ice-Cream Cone"—and it worked. As I wrote the story, I felt the emotions my characters were experiencing, and that's always a good sign. When that happens, I know I'm writing something meaningful.

So, when you're given a writing prompt that lacks creativity and seems a bit dull, I encourage you to find (or invent) something creative about the assignment. *How can you stick to the assignment description, and still make it fun to write?* When I was an English teacher, I once gave an assignment to my eleventh-grade classes. We had just finished reading *The Crucible* (a terrific play by Arthur Miller), and I gave my students an essay to write. I asked them to choose their favorite character, to describe the character, and to write why he or she was their favorite. I then gave them this cryptic instruction: "Here's the extra credit: along with your essay, *do something cool* that relates to *The Crucible*. Do something *cool*." And I grinned at them.

Hands went up, asking me, *"What do you mean? What should I do? Are you serious?"* And I just nodded and smiled, and said, "Write your essay, and then do something *cool*." I gave them a task with very little structure, because I wanted to see what they would do with it. When the papers were due, the results were very interesting. About half the class didn't do the extra credit, while the other half handed in their essays along with something bold, interesting, and profoundly *cool*.

One boy showed up to class dressed like a Puritan (which I thought was amazing). One girl gave me her essay along with five pages from a "diary" written by Abigail Williams (her favorite character). She wrote it by hand in a fancy script on cream-colored paper and then burned it around the edges to make it look old. It was very creative, and I loved it. But my favorite came from a boy who handed me a CD which he burned himself.

When I got home that day and listened to it, I laughed my way through it, very impressed at his creativity. On the CD were songs referring to angels and devils and heaven and *the other place* (thus connecting to *The Crucible*). The CD included about ten songs, such as "Devil with a Blue Dress On" (by Mitch Ryder & The Detroit Wheels); "Stairway to Heaven" (by Led Zeppelin); "Highway to Hell" (by AC/DC); and "Earth Angel" (by the Penguins). It was terrific, creative, and very original. I loved it. Easy A+.

So, when you're given an assignment that seems a bit dry and lacking creativity, do your best to find or invent the creativity there, and to enjoy the writing and the creating. And when you have your creative ideas, please *run them by your teacher first*. (This is very important: keep in mind that I'm an author trying to help students everywhere, but *your teacher is your teacher*, and is the one grading your work. So, if your teacher's suggestions differ from mine, *always do what your teacher says*.)

So, if you're craving creativity, try to *find* the creativity embedded in the assignment. When you have your creative idea, approach your teacher politely and respectfully, and say something like this: "I have an idea for this assignment. Is it okay if I do it?" And then explain it clearly. Your teacher will probably say, "That's a great idea! Go ahead and do it, but make sure you also do everything in the assignment description." And then go have fun doing it. And be sure to make it *cool*.

PUT YOUR IDEAS DOWN ON PAPER

This is a fairly common complaint among writers. You have your thoughts and your ideas, you know what you want to say, but you have a tough time translating them into words on a computer screen (or paper). There's a wall between the words in your head, and the screen where you want to write your words. And the words refuse to climb the wall and jump onto the screen. I get it.

Fortunately, I can give you some suggestions that work very well. When I sit down and tutor students in writing, they very often tell me the same thing. They know what they *want* to say, but they don't know *how to say it*. And they stare at the computer screen, feeling frustrated and demoralized. When this happens, here's what I do. I turn off the monitor (literally), or I turn over the notes, or I hide the assignment description (or all three). I remove anything that might distract the student or interrupt their thought process. And then I say this, in a very conversational tone of voice:

"Okay, let's say I'm your friend, and we're hanging out in the cafeteria, eating potato chips and drinking iced tea. You want to talk about this paper you have to write, so I ask you a simple question: 'What do you want to say in your paper?' So, what would you say to your friend? Not to me; to your *friend*. Think about what you would say, and then just say your ideas *out loud*."

And then I say, "*Talk* your ideas to me," and I wait quietly. Here, the student takes a few seconds, looks into the distance, and begins to say his stubborn ideas out loud, in his natural speech rhythms, just the way he normally talks. He rambles for ten seconds or so, but eventually expresses his thoughts clearly. This is the goal. This is what I'm looking for, and *it always works*.

When the student finishes speaking, I say, "That was *perfect*; now *write it down* before you forget it." When the student writes it down, I look at what he wrote, and it always sounds clear and natural. And I say, "Good job. That's the way it's done."

Now, think about what I just did with the student. I harnessed the powers of his natural speech rhythms, and I converted this mysterious thing—this *paper*—into natural language. And why did I do this? I did it because it's a very powerful technique, and it works. Think about all the words you produce. We *speak* a certain number of words, and we *write* a certain number of words. The number of words you *speak* is probably about 95 percent of the words you produce. The number of words you *write* is perhaps 5 percent of the words you produce (and probably even less).

This means that you have much more experience *speaking* words than writing them. We all speak better than we write, and this is because we get more *practice* at speaking than writing. Speaking comes naturally to all of us; writing is a bit more foreign. When writing words is difficult, *talk them out loud*.

Here is another variation of this exercise (and I use it myself sometimes, when I'm writing). Let's say you're writing alone, in your room with the door closed, and the words just won't flow. Here's what you do: shut off the monitor, or turn your chair away, or shut your eyes (or all three), and speak out loud, right there, in the silence of your room. *Talk* your ideas out loud until you make sense, and *listen to what you say. Speak out loud until you say what you want to say.*

And when you *do* say it, *write it down quickly*, before you forget it. It will be awesome. Don't be embarrassed when you do this; no one will hear you. And if they do hear you, just say this: "Yes, I'm talking to myself, because I love talking to interesting people." I use that one all the time, and it always gets a laugh.

Let me recap this technique, because it's very effective, and I want to make sure you understand it. When the words won't flow, turn off the monitor, speak your ideas out loud, and keep talking your ideas into the space in front of you. Say them over and over until your words sound like what you want to write, and then *write them down before you forget them.* It works.

And now, I want to give you another technique that grows out of that idea, and expands it. When you are writing your *first draft*, I want you to *write the way you speak.* This is very effective, so allow me to emphasize it:

When writing your first draft, *write the way you speak.*
When writing your first draft, *write the way you speak.*
When writing your first draft, write the way you speak.

Some teachers may disagree with this, but they are *wrong.* When you write the way you speak, you unlock the words and ideas inside you. You harness the power of your speech and your natural voice, you retain your identity as a writer, and the words will flow much faster and easier. It works like a miracle, it helps to prevent writer's block, and I do it all the time.

Let me pause for a moment, because I want to be very clear about something. You will write the way you speak *only when writing your first draft.* Later, when your first draft is complete, you will edit your writer's voice to make it sound more formal and "scholarly." However, you will retain much of what you have written, and the unique quality of your individual writer's voice will remain. Let me summarize these important points: as you compose your first draft, *write the way you speak*. Later, edit your writer's voice until it sounds more formal and academic.

And now, I'm going to give you another technique to use as you compose your first draft. Listen carefully:

Ideas first—words later.
Ideas first—words later.
Ideas first—words later.

Here's what I mean. When you begin writing your first draft, don't worry about how "polished" your essay sounds. *It's supposed to sound rough.* That's why a first draft is often called a "rough draft." *Get your ideas down first, and don't worry about how the words sound.* Write your ideas in an order that makes sense (this is called *organization*), and keep your writing clear and simple. Later, during the *editing* process, you will make your words sound more academic and polished.

Again, write your *ideas* down first, and fix the *words* later. *Ideas first; words later.* When Michelangelo sculpted a masterpiece out of Carrara marble, it started out as quite *rough*, and ended as beautifully *polished*. The same with your writing. Rough ideas *first*; polished words *later*. The process of polishing your words is called *editing*, and it is extremely important. The editing process is where a "C" paper becomes an "A" paper (or an "A+" paper). *You must carefully edit everything you write.*

REVISE AND EDIT EVERYTHING YOU WRITE

To edit your essay, read through it slowly and carefully, correcting errors and fixing things that need to be fixed. And now, let's look at this process more closely. You may have heard the term "revising and editing," but you probably don't know the difference between the two. Well, here it is: *revising is "bigger" than editing*. Because revising is bigger than editing, you must always do this:

Revise first, edit later.
Revise first, edit later.
Revise first, edit later.

To begin the process of *revision*, read through your essay several times, from start to finish. As you read, look for *problems* (not just mistakes) and correct them. *Revision* is where you fix all the *big* stuff.

When revising, you can move paragraphs, add paragraphs, and delete paragraphs. You can expand the elements that are working, and you can reduce (or eliminate) the elements that are not working. You can (and should) improve the organization and the focus of your essay. If something doesn't belong, *delete it*. You can write a new introduction or conclusion, and you might choose a new title for your essay. Ask yourself, *does this paper say what I want it to say? Is it organized? Is it clear? Will the reader understand it?* Your goal is to fix all the big stuff that need fixing, and that is called *revision*. When you finish revising, it's time to *edit*.

When you edit your essay, you fix the *small* stuff. Again, read your essay (over and over) and look for problems. Be sure to correct errors in spelling and punctuation. If something doesn't sound right, change it. If something is wrong, fix it. Learn how to spell "definitely" and "defiantly" (auto-correct often confuses the two words). If two sentences are too short, join them together to form a single longer sentence. If a certain word is not accurate, replace it with a better word. If you spot an error in grammar, fix it. Look for mechanical errors, such as a word missing from a sentence, or the same word repeated twice. *Fix it, fix it.* Editing is where you fix the "small" stuff. And here are some commonsense tips to help you with your revising and editing:

Read your entire paper over and over, until you don't see anything else to change. And how many times should you read it? At least twenty times.

To make your voice sound more *formal*, omit contractions such as "can't" and "isn't." Also, don't use first-person pronouns, such as "I" and "me." But check with your teacher on these formalities. Some teachers will allow them, and some won't.

When you feel your paper is nearly complete, read it *out loud* to yourself, slowly and carefully, and see how it sounds. You can also have someone else read it to you. Very often, our ears detect errors that our eyes have missed.

Edit over the course of *several days*. You cannot successfully edit a paper in a single day. Every day that you look at a paper, you will find errors that you missed the day before. I have found this to be true 100 percent of the time.

Here is a technique original to me, that I have never read (or heard) anywhere else. When I was in grad school, I noticed that the first half of my papers was always stronger than the second half. This baffled me, until I finally solved the mystery. When I was editing my papers, my mind was *fresh for the first half, but tired for the second half*. When I reached the second half of my papers, I began reading more quickly, skimming, and missing errors. So, I divided the first half from the second half, and forced myself to *read each half independently*. Very often, I would begin editing by *reading the second half of my paper first*. It felt unnatural, but it worked. Eventually, the second half of my papers was as good as the first half. So, divide your papers into a first half and a second half, and then take turns reading (and editing) each half by itself.

When your think your paper is finished, print out a *paper copy* (this is called a "hard copy"), and go through it once or twice more. Read with a *pencil* in your hand, and flag the errors you find. Reading your words on paper (rather than on a computer screen) provides a new perspective, and you will definitely find errors you missed before.

If you write something and it's just *not working*, the answer is almost always *make it simpler*. If that doesn't work, *make it shorter*. If that doesn't work, make it *both*.

And that's enough for this chapter. Go take a break, and do something fun. I'll see you in chapter 2.

CHAPTER 2

Teens Learn

Read Books and Make Outlines

READ BOOKS—LEARN TO WRITE—FALL IN LOVE

I want to start this chapter by talking about *books*. Books are the most wonderful things in the world, and they are waiting for you. They are never too tired, or too busy, and they never have better things to do. They don't judge you; they don't get mad at you; they won't gossip or start rumors about you. They won't kick you out of a group, and they won't leave you for somebody "better."

They'll become your friends if you let them, and if you read them closely, they will teach you the secrets of life. Wait; I know what you're thinking: *I don't like to read! And I don't like the books we read in school!* Well, if you don't like reading books, then you are *reading the wrong books*. And that means it's time to start reading the *right* books.

I promise you, there are lots of books out there that you will absolutely love. They were written for *you*, and they will change your life for the better. This has happened to me many times. *The Phantom Tollbooth*, by Norton Juster. *The Black Stallion*, by Walter Farley. *The Martian Chronicles*, by Ray Bradbury. *A Wrinkle in Time*, by Madeleine L'Engle.

Each one of those is a masterpiece, and you should read all of them. I read the first two in third grade, and the last two in seventh grade, and they have stuck with me all throughout my life. I reread them every few years, and I love them just the same, and reading them is like revisiting my childhood and awakening all the joys that lie sleeping there.

So, as part of your development as a writer, I want you to start reading (and enjoying) books *on your own*, when you're not in school. And I know what you're wondering: *What books should I read?* I suggest you start by reading *young adult* books (often called YA). These books are pretty much intended for grades seven and eight, but don't be put off by that. They are *fantastic*, and they are among the best things being written and published today. They are always high interest, are designed to intrigue young minds, and their purpose is to teach valuable lessons to young people. And they do it all extremely well.

I still read YA books quite often, and I love them. But which ones should you read? Read the ones I suggest in this book, and read the ones that you find interesting. Go to the YA section in your library, or in a bookstore. Pick up a book that catches your attention. Read the title and the author, and look closely at the picture on the cover. But don't just look at the picture—*read* it. What does the picture tell you about the story? What does it tell you about the characters? How does it make you feel? Can you see *yourself* in the story?

Next, turn the book over, and read the summary on the back cover. Then read the book's first page or two. *Do you like the author's voice and writing style? Do the words flow into your mind and into your heart?* At this point, if you think you will like the book, you will *love* it, so take it home with you and start reading it and prepare to fall in love with it.

Another way to find fantastic YA books is to look at books with *awards* on their covers. These awards are usually gold or silver, and they are very often *round*, like a traditional gold or silver medal. Gold indicates the *winner* of a particular year, while *silver* indicates "honor" books that nearly won the award. (They came in second place, which means they are *outstanding*.)

These awards are not just advertising hype; they are real, and indicate terrific books that you will absolutely love. Be especially on the lookout for "Newbery Medal" winners, because these books have been selected as the year's *best book* for young people. Having said that, books that are *not* award winners (with no medals on the cover) can be equally as good as the award winners.

Also, at the end of this book (my book; the one you're reading right now), I provide a reading list of ten books that I want you to read. Do your best to read all the books on the list, and you will become a better reader and a better writer. *The more you read, the better your writing will be.* That's how it works. When I was a kid, I read two books every week (for a hundred books a year), and that's how I learned to write. No one ever taught me how to write. *I learned to write by reading books.*

And speaking of *writing* . . .

In the introduction to this book, I said that *teachers assign writing, but they don't really teach it.* I have observed this over and over, and when I thought about it, I came up with an analogy that helped me to understand it better. Do you play sports in school, or do some other activities? Well, if you do, think about how many hours each week you put into your sport, or your club. In the case of *sports*, athletes get about *ten hours* of high-quality coaching and practice each week. (It's probably more, if we include games.) Now, how much *classroom writing instruction* do you get each week? A half hour? A few minutes? *None?*

To continue my sports analogy, this situation is a bit like a coach saying the following: *"Alright everybody, listen up. I assume that you know how to play this game, and that you're all pretty good at it. This means there's no need for me to teach you how to play. So, go and win the big game on Saturday. And, if you don't, well, that's your fault. Try harder next time."* That would *never* happen in sports, so why is it happening in the classroom? Think about it. Writing instruction is very important, and right now, kids are just not getting enough of it. And we're sending them into the game without any coaching or practice.

I have found this to be overwhelmingly true, and I did the same thing in my first year of teaching high school English. As a new teacher, I just assumed that students had been taught to write "somewhere along the way," when they hadn't. When I understood that my students couldn't write, I began teaching them the basics of writing. They wanted to learn this new skill, and appreciated the writing instruction I gave them. This newfound insight happened when I was giving my tenth-grade students a test on the book *Fahrenheit 451*, by Ray Bradbury. I'll never forget it.

Fahrenheit 451 is a magnificent book. It's a dystopian novel set sometime during a future in which *books are illegal*. And why are books illegal in this novel? Because books (especially good and great books) teach us about the world and about people, and they teach us how to *think*. And because books are illegal in this science fiction novel, the "firemen" don't put out fires; *they burn books*. And what does the word "dystopian" mean? A *dystopia* is the opposite of "utopia." A *utopia* is a wonderful place to live, while a *dystopia* is a horrible, nightmarish place to live.

If you haven't yet read *Fahrenheit 451*, read it. If you read it in class and didn't like it (or didn't understand it), *read it again* on your own. It is a masterpiece, and I challenge you to fall in love with it. And while you're at it, make sure you fall in love with *Clarisse McLellan*, my favorite character in the book. She is beautiful (in her own way), is deeply in love with life, and describes herself as "seventeen and crazy." After you read *Fahrenheit 451*, read *1984* by George Orwell. It is the greatest dystopian novel ever written, and will never be surpassed.

Fahrenheit 451 is still taught in high school today (usually in tenth grade), and it is most often taught as a novel warning against the dangers of *censorship*. (However, I once heard

Bradbury say that the novel is not so much about censorship; it is about people watching too much TV, and not reading enough books. Sound familiar?) And what is "censorship"?

To put it simply, censorship means blocking or hiding certain forms of information (such as books) from people, because other people think they might be dangerous. And speaking of censorship, did you know that *books* are often censored from teenagers? It's true; just do an online search for "banned books," and you'll see what I mean. Believe it or not, *Fahrenheit 451* has actually been censored because of its language and the ideas it contains. How's that for irony?

Okay, back to my classroom. I was giving a test on *Fahrenheit 451*, and it included writing an essay. The prompt for the essay was this: "Discuss the theme of censorship in *Fahrenheit 451*." It was a good question, and I believed my students could answer it well. We had read the book in class and discussed the topic of censorship in the novel a hundred times (maybe more). But still, students began to raise their hands, and they all had the same questions: *What is censorship? What do I say about it? How do I answer this question?*

It was a lightbulb-moment of insight for me, and I suddenly understood the gap in my students' education. I *could* have said, "We've been over this lots of times in class, so just write what you know." But that would have been ducking the issue, and besides, I wanted my students to learn and to do well, and to enjoy my class. So I decided to help my kids, and here's what I did.

I said to my class, "Censorship means *hiding information from others*. In *Fahrenheit 451*, this is shown by *burning books*. Now, think about the major characters in the book, especially Montag and Clarisse. How did censorship affect them? How did they 'oppose' censorship? What finally happened to them?" And then I gave them the structure for their essays. Recognizing this as a "teachable moment" (even during an exam), I wrote it on the blackboard for everyone to see. (Yes, in those days *not-so-long-ago*, we still had blackboards, and they were *awesome*. And the kids liked writing on them too.) As I wrote on the board, I told my kids something really cool and helpful. Keep reading below, and see what it is.

ALWAYS MAKE AN OUTLINE . . . IT'S A MAP OF YOUR PROJECT

"Okay," I said, "here's your structure for this essay: start with a five-part outline." (As I talked, I began writing a simple outline on the board.) "Number one is your introduction. Number five is your conclusion. See? The numbers in the middle (two, three, and four) are your three *subtopics*. Your first subtopic will be this: *Define Censorship*. How is it shown in the novel? Your second subtopic is this: *Guy Montag*. Your third subtopic is this: *Clarisse McLellan*. For these two characters, tell us how they opposed censorship, and what happened to them because of it. Got it?" And the outline I wrote on the board looked like this:

1. Introduction

2. What Is Censorship?

3. Guy Montag

4. Clarisse McLellan

5. Conclusion

I'll never forget the open mouths and the lights in their eyes as my students saw, for the first time, the secrets of the essay revealed in beautiful simplicity. My brief presentation here took about five minutes of test time, but I have to say, my students all used the structure I offered them, and their essays were very good—quite focused and organized. As I graded their exams, my newfound insights were confirmed over and over: *These kids need to learn how to write. And that's exactly what I'm going to teach them.*

Now, let me talk for a moment about the basic outline I used above. This is not a model written in stone, and it is *not* a "five-paragraph essay." I call it the *five-part outline*. It is a basic structure I designed to help fledgling writers organize their thoughts and their essays, and it will help *you* get started in your writing. And now, I want to say something important, and I want you to embed this knowledge into your writer's heart. When you're writing in (and for) high school:

Always make an outline.
Always make an outline.
Always make an outline.

If you don't make outlines, *start making them*. Please understand that outlines are intended to organize your thoughts and your writing, and they are extremely effective. They are *not* intended to restrict your creativity and your original thinking. I am teaching you *how* to write, not *what* to write. An outline is an organizational tool, and it is highly effective. It is a *gateway* into skilled academic writing. It gives your writing structure, but allows for original thought within an organized and focused essay. Outlines *work*, and there is no question about that.

As I have taught writing over the years, and watched students struggle with it, I have found that nearly all of them share a common complaint. When they are given a writing assignment, they stare at the empty page (or the blank screen) and say this: "I don't know what to write." It's a terrible feeling, and it's demoralizing and frustrating. It makes you feel sad.

It's like standing on a riverbank and wanting to be on the other side, but discovering there is no bridge. Only dangerous rocks and rumbling rapids. When you make an outline that is simple, clear, and focused on the assignment topic, *you will never say that again*. I guarantee it. You will always know what to write.

In a sense, a good outline translates the assignment description into a map that shows you how to cross the river in ease and safety.

An outline is a very powerful writing technique, and I urge you to make an outline, however simple, however brief, anytime (and *every* time) you have to write an academic essay. Even when you're taking a test in a classroom. And now, let's take a closer look at the five-part outline I provide in this book. I want you to learn it and use it. If you use the five-part structure in this chapter (and I *implore* you to do this), *you will definitely become a better writer.* First, I want to talk about the *nature* of my outline structure. It is extremely flexible and allows you great choice and original thinking in what you write.

As you compose your project, your thoughts and your essay will change and develop as you write. Your subtopics may balloon into multiple paragraphs (and this is always a good sign), and you may add *additional subtopics* to your writing. Again, this model (and this method) is infinitely flexible, and it is a *gateway* into learning how to write. And now, let me explain what I mean by "subtopics," and how many you should include in your essays.

Anything that you analyze should be discussed in terms of *three.* Three is the basic number that allows us to examine something in reasonable depth. As I have said many times before, *one is an example; two is a pair; three is a pattern.* A pattern. I call this the "rule of three," and it is a very powerful writing technique. I'm a successful author, and I still use the rule of three in my writing. I use it all the time, and it is extremely effective.

As human beings, we tend to (subconsciously) organize and view the world in terms of three: *It's as easy as one, two, three. You have to learn your A, B, Cs. We talked about this, that, the other. Here, There, and Everywhere.* See what I mean? When you're discussing something in an essay for school, always try to discuss the subject in terms of (at least) three aspects. Yes, you can discuss *more* than three, but the essays and papers written in high school tend to be rather short, so I would be careful about that. Adding extra subtopics may result in brief and shallow examinations of your topic. For longer papers, however, you may wish to bring *four* or *five* subtopics into your writing. That will be up to you, and you'll grow into making good decisions about your writing.

Having said that, discussing things in terms of *three* will give your essay a feeling of depth and development. It will feel *thorough*, and you (the writer) will appear to be knowledgeable on your subject. And now, let me explain what I mean by the term *subtopics*. The prefix "sub" means *under*. Just as the word *submarine* literally means "under the sea," the word *subtopic* means "under the topic." For writers, subtopics are smaller topics that exist within the main topic.

Let's start with a *main topic*. Every paper (and essay) you write will have a main topic. It will talk about one *big thing*. It might be (for example) the *solar system*, *World War II*, or *the life of poet Emily Dickinson*. Let's say that you have been studying the *solar system* in your science class. And now you have to write a three-to-five-page paper on the solar system. *What will you do? How will you organize your paper?* The solar system is a big place, and you can't write about *all* of it. Which parts will you talk about?

To start the paper, we need to tame your swirling ideas and give them some sort of framework and organization. You can't discuss *everything* about the solar system, so you have to *choose ideas to discuss*. You will start by choosing *three ideas* about (and within) the solar system. *These are your subtopics.* Here's what I mean.

As you choose your subtopics, make sure you understand the assignment, and always keep your subtopics anchored to common sense. (Common sense is a good friend to take through school and life—another lesson I learned in the Marines.) So, ask yourself, *do my choices make sense? Are they simple and understandable? Are my subtopics related to the major topic? Am I sticking to the assignment description?* These are all good, commonsense questions to ask, and if you are unsure about your choices or about the assignment, politely ask your teacher to clarify it for you. *Politely.* Your classroom teacher is your best resource to understand the assignment, so don't overlook the obvious.

Now, which subtopics will you choose? Well, think about it: the solar system is made up of the *sun* (a star) and *planets*, right? And most of the planets have satellites (or moons). So, here are three good subtopics to use: the *sun*, the *planets*, the *satellites*. Please note that we are organizing our essay by choosing *parts of a whole*. We have chosen three things contained inside the main topic (the solar system). And when we plug our three subtopics into a simple outline, it looks like this:

1. Introduction

2. First Subtopic: The sun

3. Second Subtopic: The planets

4. Third Subtopic: The satellites

5. Conclusion

It's clear, simple, and organized, and *feels right* for the material, and for a high school paper. Now let's take a look at our second example, *World War II*. Let's say that you have been studying World War II in your social studies class, and you have to write an essay that provides an *overview* of World War II. Can you think of three subtopics to use in an essay on World War II? Keep it simple, understandable, and organized.

Well, every war has a few things in common, such as these: they have a *beginning*; they have a *middle*; they have an *end*. Simple. *These can be the three subtopics for your essay*, and this is a *chronological* approach. ("Chronological" means related to *time*.) So, we are organizing World War II chronologically by using *time*. It's very simple: *How did the war begin? What important events happened during the war? How did the war end?* Again, it passes the commonsense test, and it just feels *right* for a high school writing assignment (or even for a full-length book). When we plug the three subtopics into a simple outline (this time we are including the main topic), it looks like this:

Topic: World War II

1. Introduction

2. First Subtopic (Beginning): How did the war begin?

3. Second Subtopic (Middle): Important events during the war

4. Third Subtopic (End): How did the war end?

5. Conclusion

Now, let's think about the paper that's due in our English class, and that's on the great American poet Emily Dickinson. You have to write a *biography* on her, and it must be three to five pages long (a *biography* is the story of a person's *life*). What will you do? What will the paper be about? How will you organize your material? First, start by choosing three subtopics. (I hope this is starting to sound and feel familiar to you. If it is, that's a sign that you are *learning*.)

Wait, I know what you're thinking. You're not too familiar with Emily Dickinson or her poetry (and she is amazing; read her stuff when you get a chance), but you can still set up your three subtopics *even though you don't know about her*. I want you to pause here for a moment and think. How could you organize a person's life, in great simplicity and common sense? Close your eyes, try to think of three subtopics for a person's life, and then *write them down*. Think, take your time, and no peeking below! I'm waiting for you. Relax, and don't be stressed out. This is an exercise, not a test.

You can do it. *Three subtopics . . . three subtopics . . . three subtopics . . .*

Okay, did you come up with three? There's more than one way to write a biography, but I'm a big fan of simplicity, so here's what *I* would do: I would once again organize this essay *chronologically* by using the element of *time.* Think about it. People's lives move forward in time, and we grow from one stage in our lives into another. So, here are *my* three subtopics for a biographical essay on poet Emily Dickinson: *Childhood and Early Life; Middle Life and Achievements; Later Life and Legacy.* ("Legacy" means this: What is she remembered for? What makes her an important person? How did she change the world? etc.) (Oh, did you see that word "etc."? It's short for "et cetera." That's a fancy term that means "and stuff like that.")

And now, I'm going to plug those three subtopics into a simple outline, and this time I am also going to include a basic *title. Everything you write should have a title.* Everything. Here we go:

Title: Emily Dickinson: A Great American Poet

1. Introduction

2. Childhood and Early Life

3. Middle Life and Achievements

4. Later Life and Legacy

5. Conclusion

Do you see how simple that is? All this time, you've been puzzled about writing assignments, and now they're starting to make sense. One more example, and then we move on.

In the outlines above on World War II and Emily Dickinson, we used a *chronological* approach to organizing our ideas (and our essays), and it was very effective. However, the chronological approach is also a *sequential* approach. *Sequential.* I organized those ideas in their *sequence*, in the order in which they occurred. This is another great way to organize an essay. Everything that occurs happens *in a sequence.* Think about it:

First, *this* happened.

Next, *that* happened.

Finally, *the other thing* happened.

Here is a simple example of three subtopics created by using a sequential approach. Let's say you have to write an essay on *your day at school.* Here is a simple outline for that essay, along with a simple title:

My Day at School

1. Introduction

2. I got up and got ready for school.

3. I went to school.

4. School ended, and I came home and did my homework.

5. Conclusion

Yes, I know it's a very simple example, but do you see what I mean? I am presenting the material in the *sequence* in which things happened. Don't overthink subtopics. They are simple and basic, so keep them simple and basic. And now, let's talk about *titles.*

When I tutor students in writing, I always, *always* talk to them about titles. About half the time the topic confuses them, and we have the following brief conversation:

ME: "Have you thought of a title for your project? Because you should always have a title. Everything you write should have a title. *Everything*."

STUDENT (a bit hesitantly): "Ummm . . . I don't know if I can do that. I don't think my teacher wants a title."

ME (Stifling a laugh): "When is the last time you read something without a title?"

STUDENT (Thinks for a moment and smiles): "Yeah, I guess so."

ME: "You always need a title. Now, let's think about a title for your project."

It's sort of a humorous exchange, but honestly, I can't imagine a teacher telling a class, "Do not include a title, under any circumstances! No titles, and I *mean* that!" Nonetheless, it appears that titles are not being emphasized in the classroom, so I want to emphasize them here. *You need a title for everything you write.* It should be brief, clear, and simple, and it should include the main topic of your essay. Listen carefully now: *Your title should tell the reader exactly (and in simple terms) what your paper is about.*

Don't keep your reader guessing. Don't try to sound artsy and abstract; there's no reason for that. In a way, the title is like a miniature version of your project. And now I'm going to give you a valuable tip, so listen closely: Because the title is your project in miniature form, *write the title after you finish writing your essay.* Did you catch that? Let me say it again: *Write the title after you finish writing your essay.*

Why is this a good idea? Because you don't really know what your project is about *until you finish writing it.* At that point, you will really understand what your essay is about. And that makes it the best time to choose a title. Until then, you can use a "working title." A *working title* is a temporary title that is probably going to change later. It's a placeholder until you choose the final title, and it will help keep your thoughts focused.

Okay, a little more information about titles. When I compose titles for books or scholarly articles, I usually have *two parts* to the title: the *main title* and the *subtitle*. The main title is the main subject being discussed. The subtitle is *what I'm saying about it*. And a colon separates the two. Here is a simple format for titles:

Main Topic: This Is What I'm Saying about My Main Topic

Notice that my title is not underlined, and it's not in bold. Nothing fancy; just a title centered on my paper. Now, let's look at a few examples. Think back to the three essay topics we discussed earlier: *the solar system, World War II, Emily Dickinson*. Let's try to think of working titles for all three. Let's say our science teacher wanted us to write a brief overview of the solar system. Here is a good title to use: The Solar System: A Brief Overview. It's simple, but it's accurate and it works.

Let's say our social studies teacher asked us to write a brief overview of World War II. Here is another good title to use: World War II: A Brief Overview. Let's say our English teacher asked us to write a biography of American poet Emily Dickinson. Here is a good title to use: Emily Dickinson: A Great American Poet. It's the one we used above, so here is another one: Emily Dickinson: The Life of a Poet.

All of those are very good titles, so think about the format I showed you: *Main subject* first; *what you're saying about it* second. It works very well. But you don't need to use this two-part format every time. You might use a single phrase that sounds something like these examples: A Brief Overview of the Solar System. A Brief Overview of World War II. The Life of Emily Dickinson. Those are all good titles, and they tell the reader exactly what the paper is about. But whatever format you use, remember to *create your title last,* keep it brief and simple, and make sure it tells your reader exactly what your paper is about.

And now, I want to tell you about something very important: *how to develop your subtopics into paragraphs.* This is crucial for your growth as a writer. Pay close attention, because I really want you to understand this process.

Let's say you have your three subtopics in place, and your outline is starting to take shape. It's not finished yet. You have to expand your outline and add to it. You have to add more ideas to it, more details, and more things to talk about. Your goal is to make a map of your essay from start to finish. To do this, you must develop each subtopic. All three of your subtopics must be developed in greater depth, and it's not as difficult as it sounds. But how do you do this? I am going to show you that now.

Each of your subtopics is a *basic idea* that needs to be developed and expanded and turned into *paragraphs.* To convert your subtopics into paragraphs, you are going to once again use the rule of three. In this case, you will develop each subtopic by *breaking it down into three smaller parts.* We are going to call these three smaller parts *examples.* Listen carefully: *you will discuss each subtopic in terms of three examples.* Here's what I mean.

Let's go back to our first topic, the solar system. Here is the simple outline we used, with its three subtopics:

1. Introduction

2. First Subtopic: The Sun

3. Second Subtopic: The Planets

4. Third Subtopic: The Satellites

5. Conclusion

Now, let's explore (and explain) each of those subtopics in detail. Our job now is to choose *three examples* to discuss for each subtopic (for a total of nine examples). As we choose our three examples for each subtopic, we will keep our investigation simple, related to the subtopic, and anchored to common sense. When developing your examples, here is a tip: when possible, start with a *definition* (make that your first example). *Tell the reader what the thing is.* After that, ask yourself questions about the subtopic.

In the first subtopic, we're talking about *the sun*. You see it every day, but what do you really know about it? Wonder about the sun, and ask yourself simple questions about it. *What is the sun? How hot is it? How big is it? How old is it? How does it keep us alive?* These are all good questions, and where will you get your answers? From your textbooks; from reading about the sun, and from asking your science teacher for help.

And now, from those few questions (and a little research), we are going to create our three examples. On an outline, that subtopic (with its three examples) will now look like this:

First Subtopic: *The Sun*

    a. Define "the sun."

    b. Describe the sun.

    c. Describe how the sun helps the earth (and its inhabitants).

See that? It's simple, and it makes sense. And now, let's talk about our second subtopic, *planets*. Remember, our goal is to come up with three examples to discuss about planets. Start with a definition, and then wonder about planets. *What is a planet? How many are in our solar system? How do they move? The earth is a planet, right?* Because the earth is a planet, we can talk about it. On an outline, that subtopic and examples will look like this:

Second Subtopic: *The Planets*

    a. Define "planet."

b. There are eight planets in our solar system. Name them and talk about them.

c. The earth is a planet. Talk about it.

Now, let's look at the final subtopic, the satellites. Again, start with a definition, and then wonder about these icy children who circle their parent planets forever and for eternity. *What is a satellite? How many satellites (if any) does each planet have? The earth's satellite is called the moon, right?* Well, that's related to the subtopic, so talk about the moon. On an outline, that subtopic with its three examples will look like this:

Third Subtopic: *The Satellites*

a. Define "satellite."

b. Which planets in our solar system have satellites? Talk about them.

c. The earth's satellite is called the moon. Talk about it.

And now, let's put it all together into a single, beautiful outline of our project (which includes a working title):

The Solar System: A Brief Overview

1. Introduction

2. First Subtopic: *The Sun*

   a. Define "the sun."

   b. Describe the sun.

   c. Describe how the sun helps the earth.

3. Second Subtopic: *The Planets*

    a. Define "planet."

    b. There are eight planets in our solar system. Name them and talk about them.

    c. The earth is a planet. Talk about it.

4. Third Subtopic: *The Satellites*

    a. Define "satellite."

    b. Which planets in our solar system have satellites? Talk about them.

    c. The earth's satellite is called the moon. Talk about it.

5. Conclusion

This outline is very clear and effective, and would work very well for a project of this nature. I really want you to study the outline and understand it, and how it was made. Read it slowly and carefully twenty times or so. Notice its construction. Notice how it's organized. Look for the three subtopics, and see how each subtopic is broken down into three smaller examples. Look at how the introduction and conclusion go before and after the subtopics, like bookends. It's a perfect outline for this project. It's a map of your essay, and it won't let you down.

Creating a detailed outline like this is an important step on your journey to becoming a skilled writer. There is *no way* you can look at that outline and state the eternal complaint of fledgling writers: "I don't know what to write." And I want to say something now that's very important. I don't want you to simply "understand" this simple outline, and nod your head like, "Okay, it makes sense." I want you to really understand *how it was made*. It's one thing to look at a pretty house and say, "That's a pretty house." It's another thing to understand *how the house was made*. Let's take our new knowledge, and look at our second topic, World War II.

When we talked earlier about this essay, we gave it three (chronological) subtopics, and put them into a simple outline. Here it is:

Topic: World War II

1. Introduction

2. First Subtopic (Beginning): How did the war begin?

3. Second Subtopic (Middle): Important events during the war

4. Third Subtopic (End): How did the war end?

5. Conclusion

Now, let's develop those three subtopics by breaking each one down into three smaller examples, for a total of nine examples (three for each subtopic). In a paper like this (which is different from the solar system essay), we probably don't need definitions. Nothing there is asking to be defined, so we'll skip the definitions, and *wonder about the subject*. Now, think about the first subtopic, the beginning of the war. *What event ignited the war? When did it begin? Where did it begin? What countries were involved?* On an outline, the first subtopic and its three examples will look like this:

First Subtopic (Beginning): *How did the war begin?*

a. How, when, and where did the war begin?

b. What single event ignited the war? Discuss it.

c. The countries involved (on both sides)

And now, let's talk about the second subtopic: *Important events during the war.* Subtopics like this are very broad and require some thought. For the sake of organization, let's think about three possible examples that are related to each other. For example, *we can talk about three major countries involved. We can talk about three major battles fought. We can talk about three types of ships (or planes) used during the war. We can talk about three important people who were involved in the war. We can talk about three important events that happened during the war.*

Do you see how I'm approaching this subtopic, in terms of organizing my thoughts in a way that makes sense? Think, and choose three *somethings* to talk about. All of those above would work well, but I want to give my paper variety, so I will choose to discuss three important events that happened during World War II. (Read about them, because they are all *fascinating*.)

Second Subtopic (Middle): *Important events during the war*

    a. The speeches of Winston Churchill

    b. The Enigma machine

    c. The miraculous rescue at Dunkirk

Our third subtopic is *How did the war end?* Again, there are lots of examples to choose from, but I would probably focus on the war in *Europe* and the war in the *Pacific*. (To put it simply, the war was split into two "halves," and was being fought in different parts of the world. It is a fascinating time in history.) As I conclude the paper, I will also wonder *how the war changed the world* (which will help to give the paper *meaning*). So, the third subtopic and its three examples would look like this on an outline:

Third Subtopic (End): *How did the war end?*

    a. The end of the war in Europe

    b. The end of the war in the Pacific

    c. How did World War II change the world?

And now, let's put the three subtopics (and their nine examples) together in a detailed outline that is complete and clear and simple and beautiful, and that includes a working title. Here it is:

A Brief Overview of World War II

1. Introduction

2. First Subtopic (Beginning): *How did the war begin?*

    a. How, when, and where did the war begin?

    b. What single event ignited the war? Discuss it.

    c. The countries involved (on both sides)

3. Second Subtopic (Middle): *Important events during the war*

    a. The speeches of Winston Churchill

    b. The Enigma machine

    c. The miraculous rescue at Dunkirk

4. Third Subtopic (End): *How did the war end?*

    a. The war in Europe

    b. The war in the Pacific

    c. How did World War II change the world?

5. Conclusion

And here, we have another very effective outline. It is clear, simple, and highly organized. It's a map of your writing assignment from start to finish. When you make an outline like this, you will never again say, "I don't know what to write." And now, let's move onto our final example, the poet Emily Dickinson. Remember, she is an important American poet, and you have to write a brief biography of her life. Here are the three (sequential) subtopics we chose earlier, looking tidy in a simple outline:

Title: Emily Dickinson: A Great American Poet

1. Introduction

2. Childhood and Early Life

3. Middle Life and Achievements

4. Later Life and Legacy

5. Conclusion

Once again, we are going to choose three examples for each subtopic (for a total of nine examples). We are going to make a clear and simple outline of your project. This time, however, I won't walk you through the entire process. I'm going to make this an exercise, and *you* are going to choose all nine examples. So, get a pencil and some lined paper, and *think of three examples for each subtopic*. Start by writing the blank framework of your outline, including the letters *a*, *b*, and *c* for each subtopic. Those letters are lonely and are waiting for their examples. Starting with an "empty" outline (with numbers and letters) is part of the learning experience and will help you understand the structure of this method.

To choose your nine examples, *you don't need to read a biography of Dickinson.* Just think about the periods of her life, which are the same for *any* person's life. Yes, Dickinson is a famous poet, but she was also a human being, just like the rest of us. She was born; she did things during her life; she passed away. Keep your thinking anchored to simplicity and common sense. And let it spring from curiosity and *wondering*.

To develop examples for your three subtopics, ask yourself questions about the three periods in her life. *What are you curious about? What did she do? Where was she? What happened to her? What do you want to learn?* Do your best to write three examples for each subtopic. If you can't come up with all nine examples, *don't give up.* You are trying, and you are *learning*, and that's what's important.

A martial artist doesn't earn a black belt overnight, so *don't give up.* We all develop and learn at different rates, so don't get discouraged. You will learn. If you stick with me and my methods, you will become a skilled writer. And now, go and choose your three examples for each subtopic.

Take your time. I'll be here waiting for you, and I'm not going anywhere.

You can do it. *Nine examples . . . nine examples . . . nine examples . . .*

***

And you're back! How did you do? Were you able to come up with three examples for each subtopic? If you didn't, *try to come up with at least one example for each.* Please try your best. I really want you to understand the process and the structure of this method, and this is very important to your development as a writer. And now, I'm going to give you *my* version of the outline. While you were thinking of your examples, I was too, and here they are, plugged into a full outline, clear and simple, and complete with a working title. Note that many of the examples are presented as *questions*—wonderings about my subject (which is certainly acceptable). Here is my outline:

Emily Dickinson: A Great American Poet

    1. Introduction

    2. Childhood and Early Life

        a. When and where was she born?

        b. School and education

    c. Her childhood family

3. Middle Life and Achievements

    a. Her adult family. Was she married? Did she have kids? Was she single?

    b. Where did she live as an adult? What did she do?

    c. Her writing and poetry

4. Later Life and Legacy

    a. How did she die?

    b. What are her most famous poems? (Discuss three.)

    c. Her legacy: What makes her important? Why do we still talk about her?

5. Conclusion

Again, please read it carefully. Read it slowly (ten or twenty times), and note how it's constructed. Look at the three subtopics, and look at the three examples for each (for a total of nine examples). Note that the outline is clear and simple and deeply organized. It is based in common sense and is very *human*. And what do I mean by "human"? The structure of this outline would work for pretty much anyone who has lived in the world and survived through adulthood. See what I mean?

Also, I did something a little different here. Look at the third subtopic, "Later Life and Legacy," and look at example *b*: "What are her most famous poems? (Discuss three.)." Do you see what I did there? In this example, I broke the example down further into *three parts*, suggesting that the writer discuss *three* of her poems.

This is the rule of three in action once again. So, listen carefully, and make sure you understand this: Your *examples* can also be broken down further into three smaller parts. It's a great way to develop your ideas, but do this only when it feels right for the essay, and when it works. And in this case, it feels right, and it gives you (the writer) lots of great stuff to talk about. This example (discuss three of her poems) is so full of meaning that it could also be converted into its own subtopic.

And that concludes our section on choosing three subtopics, and then breaking each subtopic down into three examples (for a total of nine examples). Now, let's talk about writing the introduction and the conclusion. First, what is an introduction? It comes first in an essay, and it is a brief section in which you tell the reader what your essay is about. As for length, keep your introduction to *one single paragraph*. Go for about five or six sentences; that's a good number for someone who is learning to write. Your introduction should be brief, clear, and simple. You want your reader to understand the topic of your essay, and (if possible) you want to generate a bit of curiosity in the reader's mind about what you have written.

The introduction is important. It mentally prepares the reader to read, understand, and internalize what you have written. It is your *hello-handshake* with readers, and it is where you will make your first impressions on them. In your introduction, be clear and simple (as always), and try to sound engaging and interesting and confident. First impressions are very important (in writing and in life), so try to make your essay sound worthwhile to read, and try to be someone with whom the reader wants to spend time. Subconsciously, readers will ask themselves these questions: *Is reading this essay worth my time? Do I want to hang out with this writer for a little while?*

And now, let's apply the rule of three to introductions. The following model won't work for every introduction you write, but it will work for some of them, and it will help you to learn and understand introductions and their purposes. As always, I will keep things clear and simple. Here are the three components of a basic introduction, offered in outline form:

1. Introduction

   a. Describe and discuss the *main topic* of your essay. (This will include your *thesis statement*, and I will discuss thesis statements in chapter 3.)

   b. Briefly describe the *three subtopics* of your essay.

   c. Briefly describe *what you are saying* about your main topic.

And now, let's talk about conclusions.

Conclusions come last and they are important also. In your conclusion, you will provide your reader with a brief *look back* at what you have written and the things you have said. This will help the reader to understand your essay in its entirety (rather than as a group of related ideas), and it will help your reader to internalize and remember the most important points of your essay. We gain learning and understanding through *repetition*, so don't be afraid to repeat some of the important points you made in your essay. That's what conclusions are for.

As you write your conclusion, ask yourself, *What do I want my readers to understand about my subject? What do I want them to remember?* Keep in mind, this is your *goodbye-handshake* with your reader, so be clear and confident as you summarize your essay and as you emphasize your final points. You want the reader to *understand and remember* the things you said, and you want to leave a good final impression of your essay (and yourself) in the reader's mind. The things you say in your conclusion will echo in readers' minds after they put your essay down and walk away from the desk.

Just as we did with introductions, we'll apply the rule of three to conclusions and organize them in three basic parts. This exact format won't work for every conclusion, but it will work for many of them, and it is simple but effective. It will also help you to understand the structure and purpose of conclusions, and it will help you learn how to write them. Here is a basic conclusion in outline format:

5. Conclusion

    a. Briefly summarize what this essay is about.

    b. Emphasize the major points of this essay.

    c. What *main point* or "lesson" do you want the reader to learn, or remember?

As you work on learning (and creating) your introductions and conclusions, keep in mind that they are a bit similar to each other. The introduction states what you are writing about, and the conclusion states what you have written about. Nonetheless, although the subject matter in both is similar, *you must present them differently.* When you reach the conclusion, you may be tempted to "recycle" the introduction, but don't do it. This will be redundant and repetitive in the reader's mind, and the reader will lose faith in you as a thinker and writer. So, make your conclusion brief, memorable, and different from the introduction. It should be one paragraph long, and about five or six sentences (roughly the same length as your introduction). Say something new, and express (in simplicity) the things you want your reader to understand and remember. And now, I want to say something very important, so please pay attention.

As I discussed the structure of the five-part outline (and how to make one), you may have noticed that I didn't start by discussing the introduction. This was *intentional,* and for a very good reason. Please slow down here and understand what I'm about to say. When you write an essay or paper for school, *do not start by writing your introduction. Start by writing your subtopics first,* and *write your introduction last.* This is a very powerful technique, and I use it for everything I write and publish.

And why is this important? Because *you don't know what a piece of writing is truly about until you have completed it.* You don't truly know what your essay is really about until you have taken your subtopics and their examples and converted them into complete paragraphs. When you have done this, you have written the backbone of your essay, and your job is nearly finished. (Some call this the "body" of the essay; I call it the *middle section.*) When the middle section is full and complete, *then* you will write the conclusion, and then the introduction. Remember:

Write the introduction last.
Write the introduction last.
Write the introduction last.

Think about it: how can you "introduce" something that doesn't yet exist? You could scrabble your way through it, but it won't be a great (or accurate) introduction, and it won't be your best work. Again, *always write your introduction last.* Here is an outline of *the order* in which you should write your essays:

1. Write a *working title* of your essay. (This will change later.)

2. Write your three subtopics.

3. Write the conclusion.

4. Write the introduction.

5. Choose a final title.

And now, I want to tell you a little secret that I learned through my experience as a writer. As you start writing and converting your outline into sentences and paragraphs, your essay will begin to "speak" to you, and you must learn to listen to what it says. It's an amazing thing when it happens. It will tell you what is working, and what is *not* working. It will inform you about problems in organization. It will tell you what needs to be deleted (or minimized), and what needs to be included (or expanded). The more you write, the more the essay will speak to you.

This conversational *give-and-take* between you and your essay takes time to develop, so you must quiet your spirit and listen to your paper, as if you're learning a new language. And, in a sense, you are. But think about this as you're writing, and listen to your essay, because I promise it will happen, and it will improve your writing. After all, you are deeply connected to the things you write. And now I want to tell you about three things to always include in your scholastic essays.

When you write your projects for school, there are three ingredients that you must include in all your essays. I call these the "big three," and here they are: *topic, focus, organization*. All three are extremely important, and if your essay is lacking any one of them, it won't be a good essay. But here's the good news: Although they are very important, they are also very simple. And now, I will talk briefly about each one, because you need to know this.

1. *Topic.* Let me start by giving you the best, most powerful, and simplest writing advice you will ever receive. And here it is: *Every piece of writing must be about something*. Did you get that? Everything you write must be about *something*, and we call that thing the *topic*. It is deceptively complex. Remember the college students I told you about in the introduction, who didn't know what their papers were about? They didn't understand the topic. As you write your essays, you must *understand the assignment* and what it's asking you to do. You must *know the topic* before you can write about it.

And now, I'm going to give you a very important tip, and I want you to remember this, and *use* it. When you know the topic of your paper, you should be able to *say it out loud in one single simple sentence.* I cannot emphasize this strongly enough. Yes, you should be able to *talk to people* and tell them, in one simple sentence, what you're writing about. *One simple sentence.* And they should be able to understand it. Let me give you some examples. Let's say that someone asked you, *So, what are you writing about?* You might say one of these:

I'm writing an overview of the solar system.

I'm writing an overview of World War II.

I'm writing about the life of Emily Dickinson.

Next time you're writing a paper, I want you to do something. Turn the assignment description over, look away from the computer (or just close your eyes), and answer this question: *What is your paper about?* If you ramble in circles, if you falter and mumble, if you speak a jumble of sentences, if you slide into silence as you search for the "perfect" words to describe your topic, then you don't really know what you're writing about. Here is a real-world example, this time from me:

Question from a student: Dr. Horan, what is your book about?

Answer from me: It's about teaching teenagers how to write.

See how simple that is? As you can see, I definitely know what this book is about. And I want to say it again, for emphasis: *Every piece of writing must be about something.* So, find that something, *find its simplicity,* understand it, and then try to *say it out loud* in one single simple sentence. If you can't do this, then you don't really know what you're writing about.

2. *Focus.* Focus comes *after* you understand the topic of your paper, and you must *build focus into your outline.* Once you truly understand what you're writing about, you must keep your entire essay *focused solely on that topic.* This means that you stick to your topic, and don't write about anything else. So, as you construct your outline, make sure it stays focused on the main topic. But focus is not as restrictive as it sounds. If you want to tell a story, and it relates somehow to your main topic, then tell the story in your essay. Afterward, if you find that the story looks (or feels) out of place in your essay, delete it. If *your essay* tells you that the story is not working, delete it.

Everything you write must somehow contribute to the topic being discussed. This is called *focus*, and it must be a part of everything you write for school. *Know your topic, stick to it, and don't write about anything else.* Don't go off on an unrelated tangent, even though it interests you. You can put it in a future paper. And please note that a well-constructed outline will keep your thoughts and your writing focused on the topic of your essay. When you truly understand the topic of your essay, *that's* when you make an outline.

3. *Organization.* This means presenting your ideas in an order that makes sense to you and (especially) to your reader. Your ideas should flow smoothly from one to another, and the arrangement of your ideas should "make sense." Your reader should be able to understand the progression of your ideas (from one to another), and not be confused by what you say.

Your ideas should proceed logically, and nothing should feel "out of place." The goal here is to write an essay that moves easily from one point to another. It should not "jar" the reader. Your writing should be easy to read and understand, and your ideas should proceed comfortably and intuitively. Your subtopics should build on each other and create a sense of understanding in the reader's mind. As we saw above, the organization may present *parts* of the main topic (the sun, the planets, the satellites); it may be *chronological* (rooted in time, as we saw in the World War II essay); it may be *sequential* (*before*, *during*, and *after*, as we saw in the Emily Dickinson essay). A well-constructed outline helps greatly with organization. However, if the organization isn't working for some reason, alter your outline until it feels right. You'll know it when you see it.

I started this chapter by talking about books. I discussed some of the books I have read, how to choose books you will love, and how reading will improve your writing. I want you to read a lot and to enjoy what you read, and I really want you to fall in love with reading. Read lots of young adult books, because they are *fantastic*. I adore them, and they will help you improve as a writer. I also talked about some of my own experiences as a teacher, and how they led me to teach my students the basics of writing.

Perhaps most important, I talked about outlines and their effectiveness. I said that you should always, *always* make an outline when writing essays for school, and then I showed you how to do it. Again, please keep in mind that the outline format I showed you is not written in stone. It is *flexible* rather than constrictive, and it allows for great freedom of thought. It is a method to help you organize your ideas and get you *writing*. It is *extremely* effective, and I urge you—I *implore* you—to make an outline for *all* your academic essays.

Remember, as your writing improves and your essay and your ideas take shape, you can modify the outline. Change the order of your ideas; add more subtopics; delete things that aren't working. The outline I provided in this chapter is a marvelous *gateway* into learning how to write. It will guide you in your writing, and it will help you understand the structure and function of academic essays—and it *works*. And now, before I conclude this chapter, I want to show you a blank outline to help you understand this process and help get you started as you grow into a writer. When we put all the pieces of the puzzle together, it looks like this:

Working Title (include the subject)

1. Introduction (one paragraph; write this last)

    a. Describe and discuss the *main topic* of your essay. (This will include your *thesis statement*, and I will discuss thesis statements later in this book.)

    b. Briefly describe the *three subtopics* of your essay.

    c. Briefly describe *what you are saying* about your main topic.

2. First Subtopic

    a. First Example

    b. Second Example

    c. Third Example

3. Second Subtopic

    a. First Example

    b. Second Example

    c. Third Example

4. Third Subtopic

    a. First Example

    b. Second Example

    c. Third Example

5. Conclusion (one paragraph)

    a. Briefly summarize what this essay is about.

    b. Emphasize the major points of this essay.

  c. What *main point* or "lesson" do you want the reader
     to learn, or remember?

The five-part outlines I showed you in this chapter are
extremely effective, so please learn them and use them. They will
assist you tremendously in your writing. And remember, the outlines you make are not written in stone; they are infinitely flexible, and they allow for original thought and creativity. They will
change and grow as you write your paper, just as *you* are changing
and growing—as a student, as a writer, and as a person. And that's
it for chapter 2. Go and take a break, get a bite to eat, or get some
sleep. I'll see you in chapter 3.

Teens Talk

How Did You Cope with the Difficulties of Writing?

OUR TEENS ANSWER QUESTION 2

In this chapter, I provide the students' responses to the second question I asked them: *How did you cope with the difficulties of writing in high school?* I knew that writing for school was difficult for them, so I asked them how they managed their difficulties, and how (and where) they did well with their writing. Their responses were very interesting. I learned about their challenges, their coping strategies, and their occasional triumphs. And now I'm passing this information along to you, so that you can learn from their struggles and how they managed to do well.

The students' responses are below. After each response, I discuss the things they said, interpret their ideas, and offer highlights that will help you become a better writer. In the second half of this chapter, I discuss the nature of academic papers, essential questions, and thesis statements. I chose those subjects very carefully, and wrote them so that you can more deeply understand the writing you do for school. It's a glimpse backstage, and you will find it very revealing. And now, here are the students' responses about coping with the difficulties of writing in high school, along with the successes they achieved.

STUDENT RESPONSES
Annabelle (Eleventh Grade)

Here is my response to your second question. I enjoyed reflecting on my past writing assignments! I've never actually done that before.

I remember a few times where my writing made me feel proud and mature, in a sense. When I say mature, I mean that when I read over it, it sounds like a person my age wrote it rather than an elementary student. The first writing assignment that made me feel proud and confident in myself and my writing would have to be my research letter to get into a competitive science program in my school. One of the prerequisites in order to get into the program was to write a research paper about any scientific subject in five hundred words or below. I do not particularly remember the specific subject, but I remember the time, effort, and research I put into it.

As for the research, I didn't really have a strategy; I would just search up the subject and choose reputable sites. This seemed to work for me and I was able to finish the paper. What didn't work out would be the fact that I overabused the thesaurus. As a ninth grader trying to enter this prestigious program, I didn't know how educated I needed to sound. I realized that in order for me to succeed, I needed to rely on myself and not compare my writing with others. I know that constructive criticism is beneficial, but in this instance, it only harmed my writing. In the end, I was accepted into the program. I was really proud of the fact that my essay was strong enough for me to be entered into the program. It made me feel confident and that my writing had matured.

In another instance in tenth grade, I was really proud of a writing assignment that I concluded. I had to do a persuasive research essay defending a position in the real world. My research was on the United States Women's Soccer team and how they are underpaid compared to the men, even though they have more championships, medals, accolades, etc. It was a really interesting topic. As I said before, I really don't have a method to my research, I just conduct it.

But this time, my teacher had a format for us. He wanted us to choose only five to six articles and make flashcards with information on the alternate side of the main idea of the fact. In the end, we would have fifty to sixty flashcards' worth of research to be used in our essay. This part of the research helped me organize my thoughts coherently and I was able to be more organized, even though it took me three times as long compared to my way of not having a method. The issue with this though was that the essay had a page restraint of two to three pages. When I put all of my flashcard facts into a document, without any explanation, sentences, transitions, or organization, the facts alone took up a total of five pages. This method didn't work for me and I ended up only using thirty of the flashcards. If I didn't, my essay would have been an experiment report rather than an English essay. What helped me was taking my teacher's advice and morphing it to my needs.

One method may work for one student, but it certainly isn't a "cookie cutter" plan that would work for everyone, or else everyone's writing would sound the same! All in all, I had to cope with the difficulties of writing and writer's blocks by following guidance from my teacher while preserving my tone and methods in writing. At times, it would be hard to formulate sentences in writing or coming up with a new idea. In cases like these, I would let the paper sit for a couple of days and not even think about it. When I felt ready to tackle it again, I dove in and was able to finish the writing. It isn't easy for everyone, but to overcome it, people need to develop their own ways to create beautiful and coherent pieces.

My Reaction to Annabelle's Response

Annabelle recognized that she "overabused the thesaurus." This is an excellent insight. It's okay to use a thesaurus when you can't think of the "right" word, but using it too much will crush your unique writer's voice, and make your writing sound forced, like it's coming from someone else. Annabelle also realized that she needs to stop comparing herself to others. It's natural to do this, but remember, we all have our own style, and we grow and develop at different rates.

In tenth grade, Annabelle's teacher required her to use flash-cards for a research project. As a result, Annabelle became more organized in her thoughts and her writing. However, she was still able to shape her teacher's requirements to her own individual learning style (and this shows maturity as a writer). She also learned that it can be helpful to put your paper down for a few days (if deadlines will allow), so that it can rest in your mind, and you can return to it with a refreshed perspective. This is an excellent technique when it comes to editing.

Birgitta (Eleventh Grade)

I think I've only had one or two pieces that I was proud of. One was about tasting a new food for the first time (lamb gyro) and the second was a short story. I would say that the worst thing you can do, when it comes to writing, is to fixate more on the words instead of the message you are trying to convey. Words are important, but if they clog up your message, it makes your writing ineffective.

Another piece of advice is to try to read different authors with different writing styles. The benefit of this is that you will see different ways to phrase similar things and change the way things are seen. When someone is writing, they shouldn't be afraid of making mistakes, because that's how you learn what you want and don't want. The last piece of advice is to try a diverse vocabulary. But not too obscure, so that few people understand what you are trying to say. Big words can convey certain feelings and under-tones that "regular words" can't.

My Reaction to Birgitta's Response

In chapter 1, I gave you an effective rule to follow: *ideas first, words later*. Remember that? That's how you produce a rough draft. Get your *ideas* down first (even if they sound rough), and don't worry about your words *yet*. When your ideas are full and complete and on paper (or the screen), *you have a rough draft*. It's called "rough" for a reason, and that's because it's *rough* and needs to be edited.

Editing is the time to worry about the *words*, and to make them sound polished and clear and academic. Birgitta seems to naturally understand this process (or perhaps she was taught it), and she tells us not to "fixate" on the words we use, but to concentrate on the "message" we are trying to send. This is very good advice. When you start writing, don't worry too much about how it *sounds*; focus on the *ideas* you want to convey.

After that, Birgitta tells us to read different authors. Again, this is a great suggestion. You might recall that (in chapter 2), I encouraged you to read books that you enjoy, because they will greatly improve your writing. As you read different authors, you subconsciously absorb language and the structures of writing. I recommend that all my students *read*, because the two best ways for you to improve as a writer are to read books that you enjoy, and to write.

After Birgitta encourages us to read, she suggests that we use a "diverse vocabulary." She makes a very interesting point, because word choices play a very important role in our writing. But don't reach for the thesaurus just yet, because using words that don't fit your unique writer's voice can seem out of place in your writing and feel funny to your reader. However, do your best to use a varied vocabulary in your writing, and try to avoid excessive repetition in your wording. (This is often called "redundancy.") Also, keep in mind that your vocabulary will grow naturally through reading books, which is the best and most natural way for your mind to absorb and learn words.

Elizabeth (Eleventh Grade)

Although writing is never the easiest of tasks, I've found that my best work on writing assignments (both those which get the best grades and those I am most proud of) is usually accomplished when I do not *overplan* what to write. I am aware, of course, that each and every English teacher preaches different methods of planning out one's writing. However, it seems that my best work is done when I merely have my sources and the instructions before immediately beginning to write. I usually write the bare minimum to satisfy the assigned requirements and then fit my sources where needed. If I can think of other examples or ways to drive my point further I will add them.

After I have what could be generously called an essay, I edit and polish. The main piece of advice is this: Just start writing. Don't get caught up in overplanning, or you will never start writing. It makes writing stiff and clunky. Write what needs to be said and then sand the edges (or indeed, add edges) if need be. This way, the author's voice can clearly be heard and the writing will flow and read better.

My Reaction to Elizabeth's Response

Elizabeth gives us a proactive way to avoid procrastination: "Just start writing." But proceed cautiously here, and don't start writing *too* soon, because (as Emily explained earlier) it's very helpful to plan writing projects before you start writing them. However, there *is* such a thing as *too much planning*. If you keep performing research and gathering resources and planning your paper (listen carefully now), your preparation may become an *avoidance behavior* and a type of procrastination. Do you see what I mean? Planning *to excess* can become a way to avoid writing. So, plan as much as you (and the assignment) require, and then start writing.

When your rough draft is completed, it's time to start editing. Here, Elizabeth uses a carpentry (woodworking) analogy, telling us to "sand the edges" of our writing in order to polish our words.

She is comparing *finish carpentry* to the editing process, and it's a good comparison (remember my *birdhouse* analogy in the introduction?). Edit last, but *make sure you always edit.* Editing is necessary for *everything* you write, and will improve your essays (and your skills) more than you can imagine. This is how the pros do it, and I'll be discussing it later in this book.

Emily (Eleventh Grade)

Writing does not always come easy to me, however I have had a few success stories that have made me proud. One in particular was a personal narrative I wrote about moving out of an old house in New Hampshire and into a new one. This assignment felt less painful than other writing assignments I have been given because it is easier for me, like most, to write about my firsthand experiences, rather than analyzing a book, or writing argumentatively. One of the things that worked well for me on this specific assignment was appealing to my readers' emotions through pathos. By expressing my own feelings and implementing how I was sad as I walked through each room in the house before leaving, I caused my readers to feel something as well. I also gave them a sense of hope, when I wrote about the new beginning and new experiences with my family that would follow in our new house.

Another assignment that I am proud of was an argumentative piece I wrote about standardized testing. One of the strategies that worked well for me was the process leading up to actually sitting down and writing my essay. I spent a lot of time analyzing different articles I found to help strengthen my argument, and I organized all the quotes and statistics on separate index cards. Then I laid all my cards out and grouped them based on similar concepts, and these groups eventually became my body paragraphs.

I do value the planning part leading up to the final product because with an organized mind-set I have a much easier time physically writing out the essay. I also believe that you should let someone else view your work, whether that be a teacher, peer, or even your parents. I truly value peer review and I know my own writing has benefited from it because sometimes you need a new perspective on your piece, and other times you have been staring at your own work for too long that you may have missed a simple mistake or two. Something I know I struggle with is writing about a topic that I am not super passionate about.

When I am given an assignment on a topic that I may not think is the most exhilarating, I often feel overwhelmed because I know I will have difficulty writing it. My advice in this case would be to accept that the writing style or topic may not be your favorite, however that doesn't mean you will do a bad job at writing it. I think once you get past the point that makes you feel anxious about writing, you will write more confidently, and one of the things I have learned is that the reader can tell more than you think about the confidence of the author. By staying organized and being confident you are setting yourself up for success in writing.

My Reaction to Emily's Response

Emily begins her response by talking about a highly successful personal narrative that she wrote. In her essay, she described the difficulties of moving from her old home into a new one. She provided a description of the event, discussed the emotions she was experiencing, and concluded this difficult experience by transitioning to a theme of "hope." In doing this, Emily gave her essay great meaning—for herself, and for the reader. Emily has figured out (or was taught) that personal essays should include a mixture of description and reflection. This is a terrific insight, and I will be discussing this topic in chapter 6 of this book.

Emily also describes her preparation for writing an *argumentative* essay. Before she began writing, she read (and analyzed) articles on her topic, and gained a good deal of background knowledge on her subject. Performing this type of research is known as surveying the "literature" of the field (and it is *very* helpful).

After that, she organized all her quotes and statistics on index cards. Annabelle called these "flashcards," but the two terms (index cards and flashcards) mean the same thing, and they can be very helpful with organization. (Please feel free to use index cards if you feel they're helpful, but the five-part outline format I provided in chapter 2 performs a very similar function, and is easier to manage.) All of Emily's preparing and organizing helped her to understand her topic and compose her essay. This process of reading and organizing is extremely effective, and I recommend it highly.

Emily also offered some effective tips for editing. She suggests letting someone else (such as a peer, parent, or family member) read your draft. This too is excellent advice. Other people will read your essay with a fresh mind and will spot mistakes and weaknesses that you missed. They can also tell you when something is not clear or is not making sense. This is a great idea, especially when your draft is close to being finished. Finally, Emily suggests something very mature. When you're given a writing assignment that you don't find interesting, you need to "accept" it, do your best with it, and write with *confidence*. This is very good advice for writing—and for life.

Jenny (Tenth Grade)

There are several writing assignments I am proud of. In English 9, we read *To Kill a Mockingbird*. For this writing assignment, we were tasked with answering two questions. The first was, "How does Scout lose her innocence over the course of the story?" Essentially, I approached it by a step-by-step perspective. My first goal was to find evidence of her innocence at the start of the story. Next, find evidence of loss of innocence, etc. I find writing much easier when I break things down and organize my thoughts beforehand, rather than diving right in. I know everyone dreads graphic organizers but they greatly improve the structure of your writing.

The second question asked to analyze major themes within the text. I find it easier to write about things I'm passionate about, so I chose themes I find interesting, such as sexism and ableism. I can relate to those, so this made me more engaged and made the writing easier. As for other writing assignments, this year we are reading the Holocaust memoir *Night* by Elie Wiesel. For this assignment, I had to write about Elie's shifting priorities over the course of the text. These could relate to faith, community, self, etc. I tracked Elie's loss of faith over the atrocities he went through. This writing assignment went well for me because I again didn't get ahead of myself. Breaking a big assignment into small pieces makes it much more achievable.

Lastly, as for techniques and strategies I use, try breaking things down. Break down the task and your time. Also, spice it up. Making your writing more engaging for yourself will get you through it much easier. You'll have more fun, and it will be done much more efficiently. And make sure to take breaks.

My Reaction to Jenny's Response

Jenny's approach to the *Mockingbird* essay was very effective. Before she started writing, she understood the assignment and what it was asking her to do. When answering the first question ("How does Scout lose her innocence over the course of the story?"), Jenny broke the question down into two major components: First, she found examples of Scout's *innocence*. After that, she found examples of Scout's *loss of innocence*. This is a very logical approach; it's simple, understandable, and it makes sense. When given prompts to write essays, make sure you understand what it's asking you to do, and then break it into smaller components. This makes your task clear and very manageable. Jenny also did this with her *Night* essay, and had great success there also.

The next part of the *Mockingbird* essay required Jenny to select major themes from the novel, and then analyze them. To improve her engagement with the task, Jenny chose themes that she (personally) finds compelling. Again, this was a very good decision. When you are given a *choice* in your writing, always choose something that interests you, rather than something to "impress" your teacher. Your engagement with the subject will show in your writing, and your papers will become more readable and interesting.

Jenny's process of understanding the prompt and then breaking it down into smaller components works very well. I suggest organizing the prompt into smaller tasks (perhaps three), and then putting them onto a clear and well-organized outline. When you understand the task and create a map of your project, you'll feel more "in control" of your writing assignments, and less anxious about them.

I also like Jenny's suggestion to "spice up" your writing. A long time ago, one of my professors told me to "go for a punchier style" in my writing. It was very good advice, and I still use it to this day. As you write your essays, remember that you already have (and will develop) a unique writer's voice, so don't be afraid to let it show in your writing. After all, you have lots of practice at being *you*. And one other thing: Jenny's right. Take breaks. They make writing easier, and you'll do a better job at it.

Meghan (Twelfth Grade)
The times I can really indulge in my creativity in writing is the most rewarding. If I do not care for a topic, I will not have the inspiration or drive to write thoughtfully. Usually it's an assignment when I have more leeway with the topic and comprehension that I feel good about. I love writing essays with topics that I care about, in those moments I have more words than ever. More words doesn't equal "good," but it can be more thoughtful.

When you are deprived of meaningful things for so long, you will turn any topic into one you desire. I did that often. Rarely are things objective, if you are careful enough, you can properly make the task into your own. Even if your teacher notices you did not follow the rubric, they will probably appreciate your perspective and preserve your points. Rubrics are usually just made to prevent mediocre work from being turned in; as long as it is quality work that satisfies part of the initial task, don't worry. This does not always work, it's not foolproof, but sometimes it's the only way to turn something good in.

I recently wrote a draft of my college essay, and we were given prompts that we could use. I felt that they weren't useful. I could not submit a good-quality piece through these objectives. I went a different route and I feel really good about it now.

For example, in my English class we were given prompts to help us write our college essays. Some of them included our accomplishments, obstacles, personal growth, etc. These were the more common routes to go. I felt like I couldn't differentiate myself efficiently this way. Instead, I wrote about my observations of other people and tied it into myself in a flattering way. I wanted to show my personality and individuality indirectly. If I felt bored writing about those common prompts, I knew whoever's reading those essays would as well . . . likely even more than me due to the mass amounts of essays that are sent in.

One of the more important things to me in writing is independence. There is constant media stimulation around us, literature is everywhere as well. Our minds are "corrupted" and struggle to have unique thoughts. Once you really connect with yourself, your values and your thoughts, you'll start to reap the benefits everywhere, especially in writing.

My Reaction to Meghan's Response

Meghan is a creative person who craves freedom in her writing and her expression. From her responses, I can see that she is very skilled at taking her scholastic writing assignments and tailoring them to her own modes of expression, and writing about things that interest her. This is known among writers (and teachers) as "taking risks." Some teachers encourage this, while other teachers insist that students adhere to the boundaries of the assignment description and pay close attention to the rubric. As an English teacher, I always looked forward to reading creative work from students who pushed the boundaries of the assignment. I felt that demonstrated (and assisted) growth among my best writers.

However, as a student going for a grade, you need to be careful here (and Meghan understands this). I suggest that, if you want to write something creative that differs substantially from the assignment description, *talk to your teacher*, and get her or his approval. This is a safe way to approach writing in high school, because grades are very important. However, if you do approach your teacher, be prepared to hear, "No, please stick to the assignment description." If this is the case, then you must write what the teacher wants. Many teachers will probably offer you a *compromise*, and say, "Yes, you can write about that, but you also need to fulfill all the requirements of the project."

It would be terrible if you wrote an excellent essay only to receive a poor grade on it because you didn't stick to the parameters of the assignment. However, even if your teacher requires you to adhere closely to the assignment description or the rubric, you can still find creativity in your approach to the assignment, in the things you say, and in your style of writing.

WRITING LESSONS
Understand Academic Papers and Essential Questions
I want you to understand the papers you write. When you write a paper for school, it is an *exercise* designed to train your mind in writing, thinking, logic, and (sometimes) research. It's exercise for your mind. You write papers in order to learn something, and every paper you write is designed for you to *answer a question*. This is called the *essential question*.

When you receive an assignment to write a paper, the essential question is contained in the assignment description. Sometimes it's hard to find, and sometimes it is stated very clearly. In either case, if you read the assignment description carefully, you will find the essential question. This will help you understand the project and what you have to do. There are three basic types of essential questions that you will encounter in your assignments. Here they are, followed by examples:

1. The *YES or NO* question:
   Example: *Should students be allowed to bring cell phones to school?*

2. The *A or B* question:
   Example: *Which movies are better: action or comedy?*

3. The *Open-Ended* question (this can include virtually any topic you can think of).
   Examples:
   Who is the greatest singer in the world?
   What role does censorship play in Ray Bradbury's novel Fahrenheit 451?
   What are the most important parts of Madagascar's culture and history?

Those are the three types of essential questions you will encounter in your writing assignments. Now, I want you to understand the different *types* of projects you will be writing in high school and college. No worries; there are only *five different types of writing assignments* given to students. Here they are, followed by examples of essential questions:

1. *Personal Narrative*: Here, you will discuss an important event from your own life. (These assignments are a lot of fun.) For example, the prompt might be to "Describe the best day of your life."

Essential Question (Open-Ended): What was the best day of your life?

2. *Informative Essay*: Here, you will *teach your reader* about something (or someone) important. The prompt might look like this: "Describe the Amazon rainforest and its importance to planet earth."

Essential Questions (Open-Ended): What is the Amazon rainforest, and why is it important to the earth?

3. *Analytical or Interpretive Essay*: These assignments require you to examine something closely, and to discuss what you find there. For example, the prompt might be to "Describe and discuss the impact of social media on students' lives."

Essential Question (Open-Ended): What is the impact of social media on students' lives?

4. *The Academic Argument* (sometimes called the argumentative essay): Here, you will discuss a controversial issue such as *climate change*. In your discussion, you will *choose a side*, and then argue your point. In this type of essay, the prompt might look like this: "Write a paper in which you discuss the causes of *climate change*. Is it caused by human activity, or is it a natural occurrence on planet earth?"

Essential Question (A or B): Is *climate change* caused by human activity, or is it a natural occurrence on planet earth?

Essential Question (Yes or No): Is *climate change* caused by human activity?

5. *Creative Writing*: Here, you will compose a fictional piece, such as an original short story, poem, or play. You won't get these assignments too often, but they're a lot of fun when you do. Creative assignments *don't need an essential question*, but your teacher will probably give you a prompt to help get you started writing. The prompt might sound like this: "Write a short story about a

character who triumphs over adversity." Of course, that character will be *you*.

Identifying the essential question of an assignment is important because it helps you to understand the assignment in its simplicity. Once you identify the essential question the project is asking, *you will understand what you have to do.* You will know the type of paper that you have to write. And, when that burst of joyful illumination enters your vibrant mind, it's time to create your thesis statement.

Learn How to Write a Thesis Statement

Creating a good thesis statement is difficult for most students, and it's a skill that must be learned. In this section, I'm going to teach you all about thesis statements and how to write them. When you finish reading this section, you will understand thesis statements (*What are they?*), their purpose (*Why do I need one?*), their position in the paper (*Where do I put it?*), and what they should look like (*How long should it be?*). I'm going to teach you all of this, and I promise to keep it simple. Here we go.

You must create a thesis statement *before* you start writing your paper, because the thesis statement will *guide* your paper and your writing. You will need a thesis statement for nearly every paper you write in school (except for creative pieces), so it is very important that you learn about thesis statements and understand them clearly. First, what exactly is a thesis statement? Pay attention, because this is important: *A thesis statement is a sentence telling your reader what your paper is about.* Read that definition slowly, at least three times. Read it *out loud* until you understand it, and will remember it.

The word "thesis" means "central idea," and it refers to the central idea of your paper. So, a thesis *statement* is *a sentence that contains the central idea* (thesis) *of your paper.* For fledgling writers, it should be *one sentence long.* Did you get that? Read this carefully:

Make your thesis statement one sentence long.
Make your thesis statement one sentence long.
Make your thesis statement one sentence long.

Make it clear, simple, and accurate, and make sure it relates directly to the assignment description. If I were to write a thesis statement for this book, it would be this: *Through reading this book, teenagers will learn how to write.* That's what a thesis statement looks like (except we don't italicize it). It's one sentence long, and it's simple, clear, and accurate.

Some writers compose thesis statements that contain several sentences, but don't do this yet. You are in the *learning* stage, so (for now) keep your thesis statement to *one sentence long.* Keep it clear and simple. As you compose your thesis statement, say it out loud and listen to it. *Is it clear? Is it simple? Does it relate to the assignment? Does it accurately and clearly convey your point of view? Does it describe your paper? Will the reader understand it?* You can also show it to someone you know, and ask them, *Does this make sense? Do you understand this?* You can also ask them to read it out loud, while *you* listen to how it sounds. If something seems unclear or "off" about your thesis statement, tinker with it until it's right.

What is the *purpose* of a thesis statement? Your thesis statement *tells the reader what your paper is about*, and that's it. It's very simple, so don't overthink it. It describes your paper in a single sentence. It presents the *subject* of your paper, and it prepares your readers to encounter what you have written. A thesis statement tells your readers what they are about to read, and this helps them to *understand* it. It prepares their mind to absorb new information. But where should you put your thesis statement? Where does it go?

Because you are telling the reader what they are about to read, your thesis statement should be *the first sentence in your paper.* Did you catch that?

Make your thesis statement the first sentence in your
paper.
Make your thesis statement the first sentence in your
paper.
Make your thesis statement the first sentence in your paper.

We put it there to let the reader know immediately what the
paper is about. *Don't keep them waiting or guessing.* Here is the
logic: *Before I start my journey, tell me where I'm going. This way,
I'll enjoy the trip. I'll understand it better, and I won't be distracted
by questions such as "Where are we going?" and "What are we doing?"*
Let me emphasize this for clarity: *Make your thesis statement the
first sentence in your paper.*

Now, let me pause here and explain a few things. I just taught
you to keep your thesis statement to *one sentence*, and to make it
the first sentence in your paper. This is excellent advice for fledgling writers, and will help you to understand and create effective
thesis statements. In my reading, I have encountered high-level
academic authors who use this method in their published articles.
It's not fancy. It's a simple, no-frills method that works very well.

However (pay attention now), some of your teachers may
teach you a different approach. They may say something like,
"Start with an anecdote to 'hook' your reader, and build up to
your thesis statement. Make your thesis statement the last few
sentences of your first paragraph. Make it about two to three
sentences long."

If your teacher tells you to do this (or something like it),
always do what your teacher tells you to do. Listen to your teachers,
and learn from them. The vast majority of teachers are very good.
Also, your teacher is giving you the grade (not I), so *always do
what they say.* I know this might be confusing. On one hand, I
am teaching you something. On the other hand, your teacher is
telling you to do something different. *Which is the correct thing to
do?* It's not a matter of which is "correct," because there are merits

to both approaches. I understand where those teachers are coming from. Those methods can be very effective, but they are also rather advanced, and they ask students to do something they're not ready to do. Or not ready to do *well*. It's a *run-before-you-can-walk* method.

For fledgling writers, I greatly prefer my own system. It's simple and effective, and it's a gateway into further skills and knowledge. If you have a choice, *use my method and learn from it.* I'm giving you a task that you can understand and accomplish, and it will improve your writing. As you learn my system, you will *grow* toward more advanced methods. When teachers give you a task that you can't do (or can't do well), it's frustrating and demoralizing, and the learning there is shaky and blurry, rather than firm and clear.

But again, I want to emphasize this important point: if my methods differ from your teacher's methods, *do what your teacher tells you to do*, and learn from them the best you can. However, *I want you to understand and absorb my methods.* They will help you to *understand* scholastic writing, and not merely perform a task to completion. I understand writing deeply, and I want you to understand it also. Then, it becomes a skill that you possess, and not a set of "rules" that you remember.

In chapter 2, I taught you the importance of understanding your writing assignments in their *simplicity*. When beginning to write a paper, I told you to close your eyes and answer this question: *What is this paper about?* If you can't answer that question in *one single simple sentence*, you don't understand the assignment (yet), or the essential question it's asking.

That understanding comes *before* creating your thesis statement, and leads directly to it. Once you can describe what you're writing about in one clear and simple sentence, you can easily identify the essential question. As you prepare and plan to write your paper, I suggest writing down *two* sentences. The first sentence will clearly describe the *central topic* of your paper. The second sentence will be your essential question (and it grows out of the first sentence). When you have those two sentences written down, it's time to write a third sentence: your *thesis statement.*

Once you understand what your paper is about, and the essential question it is asking, it should be easy for you to write a thesis statement. The goal here is to write down three sentences: The *first* sentence describes your paper; the *second* sentence provides the *essential question* which your paper will answer, and the *third* sentence will be your *thesis statement.* To write your three sentences, answer the following questions:

1. What is my paper about? (Write a single, simple sentence.)

2. What is the essential question my paper is asking? (drawn from the first sentence)

3. What is my thesis statement? (drawn from your first two sentences)

All three sentences are (and should be) very closely related. Here are three examples of this process. As you read them, I want you to note their simplicity:

Topic: Describe the Amazon rainforest, and discuss its importance to planet earth.

Essential Question: What is the Amazon rainforest, and why is it important to the earth?

Thesis Statement: The Amazon rainforest is very important to the health of planet earth. (Your paper will contain a *description* of the Amazon rainforest, so there's no need to provide a description in your thesis statement.)

Topic: Describe and discuss the impact of social media on students' lives.

Essential Question: What is the impact of social media on students' lives?

Thesis Statement: Social media are making students more withdrawn and lonely.

Topic: Identify the causes of climate change.

Essential Question: What are the causes of climate change?

Thesis Statement: Climate change is caused by human beings and what they are doing to planet earth.

In this section, you have learned about thesis statements, and how to create one. This is an extremely important part of writing a paper, and it takes time to learn it and understand it. With practice, however, it will become much easier and feel much more natural. Thesis statements are not mysterious, and they are a necessary ingredient for all academic writing. Once you understand them, you'll find that they are actually rather simple. Here is a summary (and a review) of thesis statements and their characteristics. Read this slowly and carefully, and memorize it:

What is a thesis statement? A thesis statement is a sentence telling the reader what your paper is about.

What is the purpose of a thesis statement? It tells your reader what your paper is about and prepares them to read and understand what you have written.

What are the qualities of an effective thesis statement? An effective thesis statement is clear and simple, and it accurately describes the central topic of your paper.

How long should a thesis statement be? Your thesis statement should be one sentence long.

Where should I put the thesis statement? Your thesis statement should be the *first sentence* in your paper. Don't keep the reader guessing.

Before we move on to the next section, I want to give you one more tip. When your paper is edited and complete, read your thesis statement carefully, because *it may no longer fit your paper.* Writing a paper is a journey and an act of exploration. Sometimes, your paper makes a turn, leads you into unexpected territory, and surprises you with things you didn't anticipate. An unexpected turn is a positive occurrence, and it's usually where you do your best writing. However, when this happens, your original thesis statement may no longer fit the paper—it may no longer be *accurate.* If this happens, edit your thesis statement until it once again accurately describes what your paper is about. And then hand it in—and feel proud of yourself.

And now, let's learn something very important that will change your writing and enlighten your magnificent mind. Let's learn to do something that you have never been taught before. Let's learn how to write a *paragraph.*

Teens Learn

How to Write Paragraphs and Academic Arguments

LEARN HOW TO WRITE A STRONG PARAGRAPH

In this chapter, I'm going to talk about something very important, and it will change the way you write. I'm going to teach you *how to write a paragraph*. Most students can generate a decent paragraph, but they can't explain how they did it, and they can't describe the attributes of a well-written paragraph. This is because most students haven't been taught how to construct a paragraph. They don't really understand the nature of a paragraph or how it should be structured. Instead, they construct their paragraphs from a general feeling, and their writing is graded mostly on content. And I'm no exception.

In my first year of graduate school, I took a very challenging course on Shakespeare. Shakespeare is my favorite author, and I was very excited. Wait; I know what you're thinking. You have read *Romeo and Juliet* and *Macbeth*, and maybe even *Hamlet*, and you have decided that you "don't like Shakespeare." I get it.

His language is over four hundred years old, and he is difficult to read and understand. No arguments there. But I encourage you to give him a chance. I spent time with Shakespeare and worked at it (thousands of hours), and the treasures I found there have no equal in all the world. He is like no other writer on earth, and the things he did are not humanly possible. But he did them anyway. I could explain it further, but this is a book on *writing*, not Shakespeare. But trust me on this one: when you're ready, *give him another try*, because he is amazing. Okay, back to my story.

So, I was taking a graduate course on Shakespeare. (This means I already had a college degree. Keep that in mind.) I had heard about the professor: She was brilliant, was a very good teacher, but was also very strict. She had once (I was told) spotted plagiarism in a student's paper and had him thrown out of the university . . . or the degree program . . . or the class . . . or something. I don't know. It was a rumor, and I typically don't believe the rumors I hear. But I can say this: in the first week of class, I could see that she was extremely strict, so I tiptoed around her, and proceeded with great caution. There was no doubt about it: She was your *teacher*—not your friend.

A few weeks later, she gave the class an extremely difficult paper to write. We had to analyze three of Shakespeare's plays, determine Shakespeare's "sociopolitical philosophy" as expressed in those plays, and write a twenty- to twenty-five-page paper on it. *Don't ask.* Having heard the plagiarism story, *I spent hundreds of hours analyzing the plays and writing about them before I read any research.* I had discovered (or invented) a system that made plagiarism an impossibility, and I still use it to this day. (Plagiarism means adding quotes to your paper, and pretending that *you* wrote them.)

Writing the paper was very difficult, but I completed it, handed it in, and felt very proud of it. A few weeks later, the professor showed up to class and announced that she had graded the papers, and she would discuss them before she handed them back. I was so nervous; I can't tell you. She quickly announced that "there were two *flawless* papers, wonderfully researched and organized. These are the only two As in the class." And she looked quite stern as she said it, and I swear my knees were shaking.

I had worked harder on that paper than on any paper I had ever written, and I *so* wanted to earn an A on it. Well, she handed the papers back, and imagine my joy when I saw that I had received an A on my paper. I was beyond thrilled. There it was, in red ink, proudly scribbled above the title of my paper. When I read her comments, they were very flattering, but she ended with a rather strict criticism: "All excellence aside, your paragraphing is inconsistent throughout the paper. Work on it."

I looked at the paragraphing of my paper, and you know what? She was right, and my paragraphs were wrong. Like a flash I realized that I had no idea how to write a paragraph. I already had a college degree with honors. *How could I have missed this?* So, I took her advice, and worked on it, and finally unraveled the mysteries of writing a good paragraph. And now I'm going to pass that learning on to you. Use it well.

I always learn from my mistakes, and one thing I learned is that paragraphs are extremely important to any writing. If your essay were a castle, the paragraphs would be the bricks that hold the castle up and help it to stand for a thousand years. Did you ever wonder why we have paragraphs? Human civilization didn't always have them, so we developed them in our writing systems.

We have paragraphs because they *help us read* and they help us understand. They give us a mental break as we read and absorb our beautiful books. When we finish reading (and understanding) a paragraph, we have finished a brief independent text, a small bit of knowledge that reveals something important in the book. A paragraph is like a pinpoint of knowledge shining in the universe.

After reading a paragraph, what should we do? We can keep reading (always a good choice), or we can take a break. We can put a bookmark in the gutter of the book, and then go have some lunch. (The "gutter" is the crease where the pages join in the middle of an open book. It's not a very romantic term, but it is what it is, and now you know.) Or, we can take a deep breath, look around the world, and think about what we have just read. And, if we have a question, we can read the paragraph once again, and see the things that we missed. Or, we can read the paragraph once again just to enjoy the beauty that we found there. (I love the patience of books. They're always there for us, they're never too busy, and they're never in a hurry.)

Long paragraphs can be difficult to read, sort of like running five or ten miles. They don't give us that break, that place to take a breath, that welcome pause before the next paragraph. Paragraphs that are too short can give a book a choppy feel. Paragraphs that are in the "just-right" zone give us a subconscious sense of order, as if all is right in the world. And how long should a paragraph be? Patience, my friends. I'll get to that shortly.

When I watch students write, I notice how they compose their paragraphs. When they finish writing a paragraph, they hit the "enter" key on the computer, and the cursor jumps to the next line (and this is a good thing). If the program (usually Word or Google Docs) doesn't indent automatically, the student will hit the space bar about five times to create an indent. This does create a basic indent, but there's a better way to do it.

A correct indent is a *half-inch* from the left margin. And here's some trivia for you: To create a half-inch indent, you would need to hit the space bar *twelve times*—but there's no need to do this. To put a correct indent in your paper at the start of a new paragraph, just hit the *tab key* once, and *presto*, you have a beautifully correct indent. I do it all the time. *The tab key*. Make it your friend.

Okay, let's pause for a moment, and see where we are. We know what a paragraph is; we know why we have paragraphs; and we know how to make an indent. What's next? The good stuff is coming: I'm going to teach you how to create a solid academic paragraph that will play a powerful role in all your papers. But before we start, I want to emphasize that this is a *gateway* into writing paragraphs. I want you to understand and use my method in your writing *now*, during your blissful journey to become a writer. As your writing matures and improves, you can experiment a bit with paragraphs, and modify the system I'm giving you. You can tailor them to the papers you write and to your own individual writing style. And now, let's learn how to write a basic paragraph, starting with the *length*. How long should a paragraph be?

First, I want you to imagine what a sheet of printer paper looks like after it's printed and full of words. Picture it. It's white printer paper (8½ inches wide and 11 inches high), with lots of beautiful black text running from the top of the page to the bottom. *Words, words, words* (that's Shakespeare, my friends). Around the text are the *margins*. These are the blank white spaces from the text to the edge of the paper, and they surround the text like a frame. Picture it. There is the top margin; the bottom margin; the left margin, and the right margin. They are all one inch wide (one inch is the default setting for MS Word and for Google Docs), and it just looks perfect. As you write for school, make sure that all four of your margins are *one inch thick*. It's correct, and it looks cool and professional.

And now, I want to tell you how long your paragraphs should be. I will describe three paragraphs: a *very large paragraph*, a *very small paragraph*, and a *just-right paragraph*. Let's start with the very large paragraph. Picture your paper filled with words. Let's call this the "block of text." The biggest paragraph you should write is *half the block of text* at most (and it is quite close to being *too big*). This will be *eleven or twelve lines long*. Do not write a paragraph larger than this (and don't write too many paragraphs this big). And, if you find that one of your paragraphs blossoms into a text larger than this, split the paragraph into two smaller paragraphs. This works very well, and I do it all the time. Now, let's talk about the *very small paragraph*.

Again, picture the block of text covering your paper. Now, imagine that block of text split into *four quarters*. Four small paragraphs of equal size. Each one is about *five or six lines long* (half as big as the large paragraph). These quarters represent the *smallest* paragraphs you should write. In fact, some writers and teachers would consider this to be "too small." Do not write a paragraph smaller than this, and don't write too many of these tiny paragraphs, either. (But small paragraphs like this are okay in moderation.) If you generate a paragraph smaller than this, you must expand it, or join it with the paragraph above it or below it. *Glue tiny paragraphs together to make a single longer paragraph.* And now we come to the "just-right" paragraph—the length you should aim for.

Imagine your printer paper covered with a block of beautiful text. Now, picture it split into *three paragraphs of equal size.* Each one will cover a third of a page, and will be about *seven or eight lines long.* Seven or eight lines long. This is the "just right" size of a paragraph, so always try to make your paragraphs *about* this length. But please keep in mind that these are *guidelines*, not mandates written in stone. Keep your paragraphs *flexible.* Each paragraph has its own identity, and wants to be written in its own way, in its own length.

As you write, listen to what your paragraphs are whispering to you, and don't be afraid to vary the lengths of your paragraphs. Playing with the length of your paragraphs (within the parameters I gave you) is a good thing to do, and will make your paper feel more varied, interesting, and alive. So, feel free to make some of them between *just right* and *very large*, and others between *just right* and *very small.* These are effective guidelines within which you can write and learn, and they look really sharp in a paper. This system will help you develop as a writer, it will improve your writing, and it will help you to understand paragraphs. And you will start to look like a writer.

Hold on; I know what you're wondering: *What font should I write in? How big should the font be? What spacing should I use?* Here are the answers: write in *twelve-point, Times New Roman font*, and always double-space your writing. *Unless your teacher tells you otherwise*, use this format for *all* of your academic writing.

It will make your writing look very professional. Wait; this is important, so let me emphasize it:

> Write all your papers in twelve-point, Times New
> Roman font, double-spaced.
> Write all your papers in twelve-point, Times New
> Roman font, double-spaced.
> *Write all your papers in twelve-point, Times New Roman*
> *font, double-spaced.*

And now, here is a summary of the guidelines for the lengths of paragraphs:

- *Very Large Paragraph:* eleven or twelve lines long (half the page)
- *Very Small Paragraph:* five or six lines long (one-quarter of the page)
- *Just-Right Paragraph:* seven or eight lines long (one-third of the page)

Now that we know the basic (but flexible) length of paragraphs. Let's learn how to write meaningful paragraphs. First, think back to the five-part outline I gave you earlier in this book. Here it is, in basic format:

1. Introduction
2. First Subtopic
3. Second Subtopic
4 Third Subtopic
5. Conclusion

Remember that? That's the basis for any scholastic essay that you will write. And now, I'm going to say something that may surprise you. That outline (that framework) is *very similar to any paragraph that you will write* (sort of like a fractal). Before we go any further, I want to tell you something that I have never heard anyone else say: *The structure of a paragraph replicates the structure of an essay.* This is my original discovery, and I'm going to pass it along to you. Let me emphasize this point:

A paragraph is a miniature essay.
A paragraph is a miniature essay.
A paragraph is a miniature essay.

Earlier in this book, I mentioned that *an essay has to be about something.* Well, similarly, a paragraph also has to be about something. Pay attention now: *A paragraph must be about one thing, and one thing only.* This is very important, and bears repeating:

A paragraph should be about *one thing* only.
A paragraph should be about *one thing* only.
A paragraph should be about one thing *only.*

That one thing should be clear and understandable, and here is your test to see if you got it right. After you write your essay, you should be able to point to any paragraph in your paper, and say *exactly* what the paragraph is about (in one clear and simple sentence, and ideally in *one word*). Each paragraph should be about *one thing*, and that thing is the subject of the paragraph. That is its *topic. Every paragraph you write needs its own clearly defined topic.*

Now, let's say that we're writing a paper evaluating the effect of social media on high school students. It's an argumentative paper, and we are going to argue that *social media are making high school students more lonely.* That's the topic of our paper, and it's our thesis. Now, think about the introduction to an essay. It tells the reader exactly what the paper is about, and it starts with a thesis statement. (As you read the following, please note that I treat the word "media" as a *plural*. This is correct, because *media* is the plural of the word *medium*.)

Well, every *paragraph* has an "introduction" also. It's called the *topic sentence*. The topic sentence is the *first sentence* of the paragraph, and functions like the introduction to an essay. In the topic sentence, *you tell the reader exactly what the paragraph is about*. Sound familiar? It should. So, let's say we're writing a paragraph in which we provide an overview of our paper, and introduce some of the ways in which social media make teenagers more lonely. Our topic sentence might sound like this: *There are many ways in which social media make high school students more lonely*. Read it again. It's simple. After reading that topic sentence, your reader knows what the paragraph is about.

After the topic sentence, we move on to the most important part of the paragraph: the middle section. (This is similar to the "body" of an essay.) If we were writing an essay, we would choose three subtopics that extend from our main subject. In our paragraph, we will choose *three examples that illustrate the topic of the paragraph*. In this case, our three examples will be these: (1) social media reduce personal interaction with other human beings; (2) they have a tendency to make us physically alone; (3) they make us feel *inferior* compared to the "perfect" lives we encounter on social media. As you provide your examples, you can also *comment* on them, and say something about them.

And now, it's time to conclude the paragraph. In an *essay*, the conclusion often summarizes the main ideas of the essay. Paragraphs are a little different. When concluding a paragraph, you *can* provide a bit of summary, or you may emphasize something that the three examples have in common. Or (and this is usually most effective), you can end the paragraph with a *transitional sentence* (my personal favorite). Transitional sentences help one paragraph flow smoothly into another. They make essays feel effortless and elegant. They prevent the essay from feeling rough and choppy, which is unpleasant for the reader. I use transitional sentences in my writing very often, and I want to use one here.

So, our transitional sentence will lead us into the next paragraph. The next paragraph is about the *ways that social media reduce our personal interactions with other human beings.* Remaining true to our vow of clarity and simplicity, our transitional sentence might sound like this: *Let's look at some of the ways in which social media reduce our personal interactions with other human beings.* See that? It's clear and simple, and it draws us smoothly and gracefully into our next paragraph. It's a very effective method to learn and to use. And now, let's put it all together, and see what our paragraph looks like:

> *There are many ways in which social media make teen-agers more lonely. For example, they reduce our personal interactions with other human beings. Very often, we fixate on our cell phones, and ignore the people around us. Social media also tend to make us physically alone, funneling us into a room where we shut the door and spend several hours alone, on our favorite social media. They can also make us feel inferior as compared to others. Many of our "friends" on social media tend to portray their lives as perfect, and this can make us feel inadequate and lacking. Let's look more closely at some of the ways that social media reduce our personal interactions with other human beings.*

That's a good, solid paragraph. It focuses on *one topic,* it has a clear topic sentence, it contains three relevant examples that relate to the topic, and it concludes with a clear and effective transitional sentence. In terms of length, it's a third of a page long, and fits the size for a *just-right* paragraph.

Read the paragraph three times today, and three times tomorrow. Read it slowly, and note each ingredient in it, and get a feel for how (and why) it works. Please feel free to *use that paragraph as a model* as you learn the mysterious art of writing effective paragraphs. And now, to help you understand these concepts, I'm going to give you a simple outline that exhibits the structure of a well-built paragraph:

1. Topic Sentence

2. First Example

3. Second Example

4. Third Example

5. Transitional Sentence

Compare this to the simple outline of an essay I gave you a few pages earlier, and you'll see that the two are quite similar. *A paragraph is a miniature essay.*

Before we move on, let's review the major points of composing a paragraph:

1. It should be about a third of a page long (but it can be longer or shorter).

2. It should be written in twelve-point, Times New Roman font, double-spaced.

3. It should be about *one thing only*, and should have a clearly defined *topic*.

4. It should start with a clear and simple topic sentence.

5. It should contain three examples that relate to the main topic.

6. It should end with a transitional sentence (that leads smoothly into the next paragraph).

Read those six points three times, and memorize them. As you write your papers for school, I want you to remember what we discussed in this chapter, and practice it. *It works*. Please remember—and use—and *practice* all of these principles until you *understand* them and don't have to think about them anymore. In the world of writing, the paragraph is the ultimate building block, and it will form a lasting foundation as you grow as a writer and construct the cathedral of your mind.

And now, let's build on our new knowledge and learn how to write an academic argument.

LEARN HOW TO WRITE AN ACADEMIC ARGUMENT

Earlier in this book, I mentioned that there are five types of papers that you will write for school:

1. The Personal Narrative

2. The Informative Essay

3. The Analytical or Interpretive Essay

4. The Academic Argument

5. Creative Writing

Of all five, the academic argument is usually the most challenging for high school students. It requires students to follow a certain format, but this format is not often taught in the depth and detail it requires. I'm going to teach it to you now, because you will need it in college as well as high school.

First, what is an academic argument? An academic argument is an essay in which you try to argue a certain point convincingly. Your goal is (theoretically) to convince the reader that your point of view is the "correct" one. If that's not possible, your next goal is to make the reader think more deeply about the issue you discuss, and to understand its view from both sides. However, your actual goal for writing an academic argument in high school is to write a convincing paper that is presented strongly and correctly. Please don't wonder and worry if your teacher "agrees" with you. Your teacher is grading you on the *quality* of your writing and the presentation of your argument—not on whether she or he agrees with your views.

But what sort of topics will you discuss? They will most likely be controversial issues that exist in the real world. Controversial issues have two (or more) sides to them, and both sides usually have their valid points. The issues you discuss will be meaningful, and should not belabor the obvious. These issues will often be "political" in nature. They will be things that people feel passionately about, and *you* will feel strongly about some of them. These are often topics that make some people feel uncomfortable. Some of these topics can be quite inflammatory, and are best avoided in "casual" conversation, like when you're at a party or out at a restaurant. Sometimes, it's best to smile and keep your opinions to yourself.

However, when you write an argumentative paper, you are required to express your views strongly and clearly. When your teacher assigns an argumentative essay, she will often ask you to choose a topic from a list of topics that she provides. The *prompt* for your essay will often be the "Yes or No" prompt or the "A or B" prompt. Here are three prompts that you might see in high school:

1. Do *violent video games* make students more violent? (This is a "Yes or No" prompt.)

2. Do *social media* make high school students more lonely? (This is a "Yes or No" prompt.)

3. Is *climate change* caused by human activity, or is it a natural occurrence? (This is an "A or B" prompt.)

And now, I'm going to say something very important. When you are given a prompt, read it over several times to make sure you understand the question, and what it's asking you to do. Next, you must *choose a side*. You must argue one way or another. You cannot play "both sides of the fence"; a paper like that would be boring and meaningless. You must choose one side, reveal it quickly to the reader, and then argue your position clearly and strongly. Let me say this again:

> Choose a side, because you cannot play "both sides of the fence."
> Choose a side, because you cannot play "both sides of the fence."
> *Choose a side, because you cannot play "both sides of the fence."*

As you grow to understand the assignment, and decide upon a side to argue, don't try to choose the "right" one, because there is no "right" side to argue. Rather, ask yourself a simple, silent question: *As a human being, which side do I agree with?* When you choose your side to argue, always *choose something that you actually believe in.* You'll enjoy writing the paper more, and your arguments will be more convincing, because they come from your heart.

When you choose your side to argue, it's time to create a thesis statement (remember, this will be the first sentence of your paper). Now, think about the three topics above. Each of them could generate *two possible thesis statements*, so let's take a look at both sides. Please note that none of these thesis statements is the "right" one; *each of them* could be used to generate an excellent argumentative paper. Here are the thesis statements for each prompt, labeled A and B:

1. Do *violent video games* make students more violent?

A. Violent video games make students more violent.

B. Violent video games *do not* make students more violent.

2. Do *social media* make high school students more lonely?

A. Social media make high school students more lonely.

B. Social media *do not* make high school students more lonely.

3. Is *climate change* caused by human activity, or is it a natural occurrence?

A. Climate change is caused by human activity.

B. Climate change is a natural occurrence on planet earth.

In this chapter, I am going to use the example of social media making students more lonely, so let's pretend we're writing a paper on that subject. Our thesis statement will therefore be "Social media make high school students more lonely." But wait. Although we have our thesis statement, we can't start writing just yet. We have to understand the *ingredients* and structure of an academic argument, because there is a proper (and highly effective) way to construct an academic argument, and I'm going to tell you about it right now. Pay attention, because this is very important. You are about to learn how to write an academic argument.

First, there are *four major ingredients* to any argumentative essay, and here they are: *Thesis statement; Definition of terms; Evidence; Counterarguments.* You will include *all of them* in every argumentative essay you write. As you write your argumentative essays, you will also use the five-part outline I showed you in chapter 2 of this book. Here is a simple five-part outline for the argumentative essay. Note that it has been adapted to fit the argumentative essay, and includes the four ingredients mentioned above:

1. Introduction (includes the thesis statement)

2. Definition of Terms

3. Evidence (and your main arguments)

4. Counterarguments (opposing viewpoints)

5. Conclusion

That's the outline format we are going to use for the argumentative essay. And now, here are those four ingredients, explained in depth. Pay attention, because this is good stuff:

1. *Thesis Statement.* We've already discussed thesis statements thoroughly, so you should have a fairly good understanding of what they are. Remember, your thesis statement *tells the reader what the paper is about.* It is clear and simple, it is one sentence long, and it is the first sentence in your essay. In an argumentative paper, your thesis statement *must tell your reader exactly what position you are arguing.* In our case, the thesis statement is this: *Social media make high school students more lonely.*

2. *Definition of Terms.* In this section, you will explain to your reader things that he or she may not understand. Think about the stuff you will be writing about, and ask yourself: *Is there anything in this paper a reader might not understand?* If so, explain it. For example, when you use the term "social media," what exactly are you talking about? Will you be discussing any particular *types* of social media, such as texting or video-chats? Will you mention *Facebook*, *Instagram*, or *Snapchat?* How many terms should you define? As many as you need to, but *three* is always a good number.

Don't assume that your reader is familiar with the things you will be discussing, or that they understand your viewpoint. As a writer, you can never be faulted for explaining things clearly. You might have noticed that I do this constantly throughout this book. Sure, some of my readers will already know the words I define and the concepts I discuss, but others won't—and I want to teach *everybody*. When in doubt, *define your terms*.

3. *Evidence* (and your main arguments). All four ingredients are important in an argumentative essay, but *evidence* is the most important part of this paper. This is where you will present your main arguments and convince your reader that your point of view is the "correct" one (or is worthy of further consideration). As you consider evidence to bring into your paper, always discuss *three (or more) examples* of why your viewpoint is the best one to choose. This important section *should be composed of several paragraphs*. As you learn to write the argumentative essay, I suggest writing *one paragraph for each of your examples*. This is a highly effective approach, and it brings me to an important writing technique.

If you are writing a *research* paper, these examples of evidence will be taken from other sources, such as books and articles. In *our* paper, however, our evidence will be based on the student's personal knowledge and experience. This paper will be argumentative, but *personal* in nature. During your time in school, you have probably heard the term "summary and commentary" (especially when taking tests). However, you're not one-hundred-percent sure what it means. Let's learn it now, because you'll be using this technique in your argumentative papers. Read this carefully (several times); it's very important.

When you present an example of "evidence," you will do two things. First, you will "summarize" it. You will describe it and explain it to the reader. That's the "summary" part. After you *summarize* it, you will provide "commentary" on it. You will *discuss* it (in your own original words), and show the reader how it relates to your argument, and how it reinforces and illustrates your point of view. That's the *commentary* part. It is an extremely effective two-part process, and you should make it a part of all your scholastic writing. In fact, it's so important that I will emphasize it strongly:

When presenting *evidence* to the reader, provide
summary and commentary.
When presenting *evidence* to the reader, provide
summary and commentary.
When presenting evidence *to the reader, provide* summary
and commentary.

And now, I will give you an example of how this should look
in an argumentative paper. Think back to the paragraph I wrote
earlier. (It was about *the ways in which social media make us more
lonely.*) I ended that paragraph with this transitional sentence:
"Let's look more closely at some of the ways that social media
reduce our personal interactions with other human beings." Now,
let's write *that* paragraph.

In the *summary* portion, I will provide an example of how
social media reduce our interactions with other people, and this
will be based on my own personal observations (presented as if
it's coming from a student). Here is my *summary*, where I explain
my first example of evidence to the reader. In the paragraph I
wrote earlier, this was my first example: "Very often, we fixate on
our cell phones, and ignore the people around us." Now, I will use
summary and commentary to develop that example into its own
paragraph. Here's the *summary* portion:

> *When I'm in school, sometimes I go to the library. Whenever
> I'm in there, I always see six kids sitting around a table. But
> they are all on their cell phones, texting or something, and not
> talking to one another.*

That's my *summary*. Now it's time for the *commentary*. Here,
I will "interpret" the example, and relate it to my thesis. I will
also emphasize how it confirms my point of view. Here's my
commentary:

This seems very strange to me. They all know each other, and they are sitting at the same table, close to one another. But they're not talking to anyone. How is this any different from being alone? If they didn't have cell phones, they would be talking to each other, laughing, and having fun.

Those two things are *summary and commentary*. I described an example (*summary*), and then I discussed it and related it to my point of view (*commentary*). Now, let's put it all together. I will start the paragraph with a *topic sentence*, and end it with a *transitional sentence*. Now, let's see how it looks as a complete and well-written paragraph:

Social media cut down on our personal exchanges with other people. When I'm in school, sometimes I go to the library. Whenever I'm in there, I always see six kids sitting around a table, but they are all on their cell phones, texting or something, and not talking to one another. This seems very strange to me. They all know each other, and they are sitting at the same table, close to one another, but they are not actually talking to anyone. How is this any different from being alone? If they didn't have cell phones, they would be talking to each other, laughing, and having fun. Let's see some of the ways that social media make us physically alone.

Do you see how that works? That is a strong paragraph that would work very well in an argumentative essay. I also used the lessons I taught you earlier. I started with a topic sentence, ended with a transitional sentence, and stayed close to the *just-right* length. The only thing different is that I wasn't concerned with placing three examples inside the paragraph. Because this is an *evidence* paragraph in an argumentative essay, I was more concerned with presenting an *evidentiary example*, and explaining it in terms of *summary and commentary*. Here is an outline for an *evidence paragraph* in an argumentative essay:

1. Topic Sentence

2. Summary

3. Commentary

4. Transitional Sentence

And now, let's look at the final ingredient in an argumentative essay: counterarguments.

4. *Counterarguments.* This is the part of your paper where you consider (and anticipate) *opposing* points of view (one or two usually works well), and then knock them down. As you do this, you will *once again use a mixture of summary and commentary*. In the *summary* portion, you will describe the counterargument and mention its strengths.

After that comes the *commentary* portion. Here, you will emphasize the *weakness* of the counterargument, or how it is somehow deficient. You will also explain why your point of view is stronger and preferable. Students usually have trouble with this section of the paper, and feel that it weakens their argument. Done well, however, it *strengthens* your argument. It also makes you look thorough and sharp, as if you have carefully thought through the issue, and arrived at a very compelling conclusion.

Before you start writing your counterarguments, do some mental preparation. Think about the *other side* of the argument, and *pretend you're writing a paper from that angle*. If you were writing about the *opposing* point of view, what would your thesis statement sound like? It might sound like this: *Social media do not make high school students more lonely*. And now, *think*: if you were writing *that* paper, what examples of *evidence* would you use?

To do this, ask yourself some simple questions, such as this: *how do social media help people to communicate, and bring people together?* Because they *do*. It's not a black-and-white issue; it's complex and nuanced, and there are good arguments on both sides of the subject. And this will be the case with *all* the argumentative essays you write. Let's take a look at the *summary* portion of one possible counterargument:

> *My friend's mom is in the military, and she's deployed to the other side of the world. But every night, my friend and his family have a video-chat with his mom for an hour. His father puts the laptop on the dinner table, and they all eat dinner together (even his mom). It makes everyone feel better, and it's almost like mom is sitting with them at the dinner table.*

It's a very good example, and it would be hard to argue with it. So, how can we use this to our advantage, and show the reader that (nonetheless) social media make high-schoolers more lonely? Here is the *commentary* portion of our counterargument, in which we place this evidence in a new context:

> *This is an excellent example of social media at its best, but it's also a rare occurrence. For most people, social media revolve around their cell phones or their laptops, and around online "friends" who don't really know them.*

And now, let's put it all together, with a topic sentence in front and a summarizing sentence in back. (In this case, I will *not* end with a transitional sentence.):

> *However, there are some ways that social media can bring people together. My friend's mom is in the military, and she's deployed to the other side of the world. But every night, my*

friend and his family have a video-chat with his mom for an hour. His father puts the laptop on the dinner table, and they all eat dinner together (even his mom). It makes everyone feel better, and it's almost like mom is sitting with them at the dinner table. This is an excellent example of social media at its best, but it's also a rare occurrence. For most people, social media revolve around their cell phones or their laptops, and around online "friends" who don't really know them.

That would be an effective counterargument in an argumentative essay. I *might* include another counterargument if I felt it was necessary. I would make that decision as I wrote the essay, and I would listen to the essay *tell me* what it wants and what it needs. And for all my fledgling writers out there, I offer you these words of wisdom: In your argumentative essays, you must include at least one counterargument, and possibly *two*, but be careful about including three counterarguments, especially if the essay is rather short (let's say five pages or less).

So, why did I end the paragraph with a *summarizing* sentence, rather than a transitional sentence? I did this because the essay is nearly finished, and the next paragraph will likely be the essay's conclusion. My concluding sentence performs two tasks: First, it concludes the paragraph decisively. Second, it provides commentary that summarizes my rebuttal to the counterargument I provided in the paragraph. A summarizing sentence like this is an advanced technique, but it works well. If you read the paragraph slowly and carefully two or three times, I think you'll understand what I'm saying.

As you write your argumentative essays in school, I want you to remember what we talked about here, and I want you to learn, understand, use, and practice the techniques I taught you. But I want to say something else, and it's very important. Earlier in this chapter, I gave you a simple outline for the argumentative essay.

Now, let's expand that simple outline into a full outline for an argumentative essay, and see how it looks in all its glory. This is a good way for you to visualize and understand the components and the flow of an argumentative essay. Please understand that this outline is based on the five-part outline format I gave you in chapter 2 (which works extremely well), but has been adapted to fit the argumentative essay. Before you write an essay of this nature, I urge you to write an outline first. This will create a map of your assignment, from start to finish. I promise you will never again say "I don't know what to write." You will also write a paper that is focused, organized, and meaningful. Here is the full outline. Please read it three times today, and another three times tomorrow:

Working Title (include the subject of the essay, along with your viewpoint)

1. Introduction (one paragraph; write this last)

    a. Provide the thesis statement.

    b. Briefly discuss what this paper is about, along with *your point of view*.

    c. Briefly discuss why this subject is important.

2. Definition of Terms

    a. Define your first term.

    b. Define your second term.

    c. Define your third term.

3. Main Arguments and Evidence (Provide summary and commentary for each example.)

    a. First Example of Evidence

b. Second Example of Evidence

c. Third Example of Evidence

4. Counterarguments (Provide summary and commentary for each counterargument.)

    a. First counterargument (This is necessary.)

    b. Second counterargument (Include this if it will assist your argument.)

    c. Third counterargument (possible, but only if necessary)

5. Conclusion (one paragraph)

    a. Restate your point of view, and how you feel it is the "correct" one.

    b. Discuss why the subject is important in the "real world."

    c. What *main point* or "lesson" do you want the reader to learn, or remember?

In this chapter, we learned how to write effective paragraphs, and we learned how to write an argumentative essay. This is very valuable knowledge, and it will help you develop as a writer and a student. It was a lot of material to digest, so I encourage you to revisit this chapter and read it carefully several times. Repetition provides deep and long-term learning, and I want you to absorb these principles and practice them in your scholastic writing. And now, let's turn to chapter 5. A group of high school students want to tell you about the successes they achieved.

CHAPTER 5

Teens Talk

What Were Your Successes as a Writer?

THIS CHAPTER CONTAINS THE THIRD (AND FINAL) GROUP OF student responses to a question I asked them. Here is the question: *How did you grow as a writer, and what successes did you achieve?* In the first question (in chapter 1), teens discussed their struggles with writing. In the second question (chapter 3), teens discussed how they *coped* with the difficulties of writing for school. In the third (and final) question, teens discuss the successes they achieved in writing. They also discuss how they grew as writers, and they offer advice to other teens who want to learn how to write.

You'll find the students' responses below, so you can see how they achieved their successes. After each student's response, I explain the things they said, interpret them, and elaborate on them. Read this chapter carefully. If you understand how these teens achieved their successes (even "minor" ones), you can learn their techniques, and become more successful as a writer. Pay careful attention to the methods they used, and to my discussions about their methods. See which ones you understand most, and which ones speak to your heart. And then, bring these methods into your own writing, and allow them to boost your understanding of how to write well.

In the second half of this chapter, I discuss how to bring research and quotes into your writing, and I discuss how to revise and edit your papers. These topics are not as difficult as they sound, and they will improve your writing greatly. And now, let's hear from these students and the successes they achieved.

Annabelle (Eleventh Grade)

Although writing certain essays and projects have proven to be difficult for me, I have had a few successes that have gotten me a good score and confidence. What worked in some of these writing assignments was listening to my teacher and utilizing their formula for writing. Because the teacher is the one grading the essay, I realized that I should follow their template in order to get a good grade. But I've learned that these formulas that teachers use aren't the same for every assignment or class. For example, in my AP English class, our thesis has to use specific examples, while in my AP history class, our thesis has to be more ambiguous and less detailed. Just like writing to a friend versus submitting an essay to a teacher, writing in different circumstances varies. A writer may use a completely separate diction when writing an essay rather than talking to a friend.

As a writer, I've grown a considerable amount when I compare my high school writing to my junior high writing. I've begun to use more complex words, sentences, and thoughts in my essays. I remember in the past I would have difficulties in formulating my complex thoughts on paper. Now I'm able to do so in a complex but understandable manner. When I head off to college, I will be sure to continue my current English teacher's method of "writing to think."

Before starting a writing piece, conversation, and/or a book, she'd tell us to go into our journals to write. Sometimes she'd give us time to write about a private choice, or she would give us a prompt. But in both cases, writing to develop a thought has helped me much more than writing without thinking. Sometimes our minds can become cluttered up with thoughts and ideas and you can only keep that organized for so long before you start to forget things, which is why sticky notes and to-do lists were invented. This is why I will continue to write to think before starting a writing assignment, so I can organize and develop my thoughts before just diving right into a piece.

My favorite or most successful writing piece would have to be back in ninth grade when I wrote a poem for the "Avalon Writers" Cabin. My English teacher informed us that there was a writing competition for the Cabin's 2020 Fall issue and she encouraged all of us to participate. I decided to participate and I like to think that the piece I wrote was the best I've ever done. It was a poem about Mother Nature and how (as a world) we tend to forget about her beauty and what she provides for us.

I used imagery, metaphors, complex words, and many other methods of development and I was entered into the 2020 issue. Later that year, I had also earned a poetry award from my school, which I was very proud of. In another poetic instance, my high school does a poem day where we all go outside and listen to people reciting poems. I had written one that was inspired by one of my favorite songs and I believe it was much better than my Mother Nature poem.

Some advice that I'd like to give to fellow young writers would be to just write. Not just in school for mandated assignments, but in your free time and for competitions. For me, I would probably never have known that I loved poetry or that I was good at it until I joined poetry competitions or wrote on my own. Not that you have to join a competition, but just write in your free time. You can write anything you want—comics, poems, narratives, biographies, etc. It is a life skill that we need to be proficient in to communicate with fellow peers. Writing is such a beautiful and expressive tool that you can use any time, you just have to develop it more.

My Reaction to Annabelle's Response

Annabelle starts by encouraging young writers to *learn from their teachers* and to follow their directions. This is great advice, because your teachers are standing at the front of the room for a reason. They are highly educated and have been thoroughly trained in their areas. This is very good advice for learning to write, and for getting a good grade. Annabelle also understands that different audiences require different writer's voices. When writing for a teacher, your voice should be more formal than when texting a friend. Keep this in mind when writing your papers.

Annabelle also discusses her teacher's method of "writing to think." Here's how it works. When starting new learning, the teacher tells the students to get their writing journals. Next, she gives them a writing prompt to direct their thoughts and lets them express their thoughts freely. This is a terrific exercise called *freewriting*, and my high school English teacher did it also.

I loved it, and I encourage all fledgling writers to try it. Get a journal, make it your own, and start writing in it. Write every day for five minutes, and see where it takes you. Write your thoughts and concerns in any way that you want to write them, and don't worry about sounding smart or fancy. Write from your heart and see what appears on the page.

Free-writing is a great way to warm up before writing. It liberates your mind, focuses your thoughts, and helps you to grow accustomed to the writing process. Before starting a paper, you might write in your journal, and consider questions such as these: *What is the paper about? What do I know about the subject? What do I want to know about the subject? How should I structure the paper?* Journaling is an excellent way to brainstorm ideas, and you'll be surprised at how your subconscious mind assists in the process.

Finally, Annabelle encourages young writers to "just write." This is terrific advice. It's simple and practical, and will help you blossom into a skilled writer. Think about it: if you wanted to learn to play guitar—if you really, really, *really* wanted to learn to play the guitar, you would practice a bit every day, and you would become very good at it. Writing is no different. Do a little writing every day.

Birgitta (Eleventh Grade)

I'm not really sure what to say for progression as a writer, because I'm really struggling with stagnation. I haven't written creatively since last year. Even then, that wasn't really enjoyable for me. I liked reading the short stories though. That may help. Learning how to not abuse long sentences is a thing I will strive to do in college. Also, trying to overcomplicate things to sound more intelligent isn't effective writing.

I think that my second-favorite piece I wrote was a postapocalyptic short story [Birgitta's favorite piece was her *lamb gyro* essay, mentioned earlier in this book]. It was based off the Metallica song "Seek and Destroy." It's incomplete, but I really liked the writing process. It also wasn't an assignment. I wrote it at the start of the COVID pandemic. I think I felt a bit less pressure when I wrote it. I oftentimes struggle with disliking my pieces and having the creativity sucked out of my work. Try writing stories based off of songs when you're stuck in a rut. I'm not really sure what the real solution is.

My Reaction to Birgitta's Response

Birgitta does very well with creative assignments and prefers them to the structured writing she often encounters in school. One of her goals (for writing in college) is to write fewer long sentences, and this is a good idea. As you write, try to vary your sentence length. Reading sentences that are all the same length has a hypnotic effect on the reader, and is rather dull. Also, don't make your sentences too short or too long. Short sentences feel choppy, while very long sentences make the reader work harder than necessary, and can be difficult to understand.

Birgitta also advises young writers not to "overcomplicate" their writing in an effort to sound "intelligent." This too is very good advice. Many fledgling writers want to impress their teachers, and try to use a vocabulary beyond their years, but this just doesn't work. Your paper will sound forced rather than natural, and teachers can spot this very quickly. Keep your writing clear and simple, and let your own natural voice tell the story.

Birgitta particularly enjoyed a creative writing project that grew out of a song she likes. Annabelle said something similar. She wrote a poem inspired by one of her favorite songs, and won an award for it. If you're interested in creative writing, but "don't have any ideas," this is an excellent way to jump-start your imagination. So, think about your favorite songs, choose one, and then write something that springs from the song. It could be a short story, a poem, or just some freewriting about why you like the song.

I find that most teens enjoy music very much, so this is a fun way for you to write about something that you enjoy. And which song would I choose? Probably "Eleanor Rigby," or "Penny Lane," or maybe "Nowhere Man," all by the Beatles. If you haven't heard these songs yet, listen to them. But you better be sitting down, because you're about to fall in love with four lads from a place called Liverpool.

Elizabeth (Eleventh Grade)

The successes I have had with writing have all come as surprises to me. I often underestimate myself and in doing so, often produce my best work. For example, in my sophomore year of high school, I had an assignment to write a persuasive essay on book banning in American schools. I wrote and rewrote the essay many times, convinced it was not good enough. Eventually, I turned it in, feeling terrible as I did so. I was sure that I would get a low grade. However, I ended up getting full marks on that assignment, with a stream of praise from the teacher.

In contrast, when I submitted an assignment that I was very sure of, my grade was not as high. This is not to say that one should question every move, but rather that full confidence in a writing piece is not an indicator it is perfect. Self-doubt is not a terrible thing in writing.

My Reaction to Elizabeth's Response

Elizabeth describes two experiences she had with the grades she received on her writing. In the first case, she worked very hard on one assignment, but felt her final draft was weak. Nonetheless, she received a very good grade on it. In the second case, she felt confident about her paper, but was disappointed with the grade she received on it.

This is very common among writers, even professional ones, and it can be very frustrating. A while back, I overheard a conversation between a teacher and a student. The student was a bit disappointed with the grade she received on an essay, and the teacher explained it like this: "Every paper comes to me with a grade already on it," which is a good explanation of the grading process. But let's say you feel confident on a paper, but are disappointed with the grade you receive on it. What do you do?

There are a few things you can do, and they are all common sense. First, work hard on your project before you hand it in. Make sure you understand what the teacher is asking you to do, and stick to the parameters of the assignment description. If you're unsure about anything, go to your teacher, and *politely* ask for clarification. *Write down* what they say so you don't forget it. As you write your paper, make sure *you answer the question being asked*. Stay focused and organized, and be sure to rewrite and edit your paper. If there is a rubric, study it carefully, and make sure your paper includes all the elements required to receive a high score. Make sure you do everything you can on your end to earn a high grade.

If you are disappointed with the score you receive on a paper, you can go to your teacher and *politely* ask about the grade you receive. You can also *politely* ask the teacher for *advice* on how to improve your writing. Teachers like when students are *polite* and value the teacher's opinion. You will come across as someone who wants to learn and excel. This is always a positive development and will elevate the teacher's opinion of you as a student.

But this is also a matter of time and experience. Keep writing, keep working hard, and your perceptions of your papers will become more accurate, and will more closely align with the *teacher's* perceptions of them. After a while, your writing will improve, and you'll be able to more accurately predict the grade you receive on a paper. And, if you are disappointed with a grade you receive, *don't give up*, and don't stop *trying*. If you conclude your journey toward becoming a writer, you'll be disappointed with *all* the grades you receive. Keep working hard, keep trying, and *never quit*. You will learn more, and your grades will *definitely* improve.

Emily (Eleventh Grade)

Although I have had struggles with writing and its process, I have also had successes. I have definitely grown as a writer from being a simple and basic writer in elementary school to a more complex writer now that I am in high school. Something that I have succeeded at in writing is being able to implement more detailed and authentic responses to prompts rather than only providing surface level information in my writing. More recently I have truly been able to understand what teachers mean when they say "show, don't tell" in your writing, and have been practicing enriching my writing with deeper thoughts. It has taken me a while to incorporate intricate ideas that make the audience dig for the main idea instead of plainly telling them exactly what the message is.

I advise students not to compare their writing process with others because sometimes it can make you question your own ideas. In writing there are really so many different angles to approach a prompt, that all your ideas may be correct. I used to struggle with more vague prompts, and I definitely prefer something straight to the point that tells me exactly what to do. However, I find that once you understand that the prompt doesn't give you clear instructions to get that A+, you can have more unique responses than other students and grow your creative mind.

I have had success at planning out my writing before actually writing it because it provides the piece with an outline of the shape your writing will take. However, if you are like me and you tend to become nervous if your writing takes a different shape than initially planned for, it honestly can become an even better paper because you are coming up with new ideas as you write that add more than your original thoughts.

The most valuable thing about writing that I have learned is you have to know your audience. For example, if I wrote a letter to a second-grade class about global warming and another letter to the governor on the same topic, I would use different syntax for each letter and include different appeals for each audience. Overall, writing is a process and it is not going to be perfect the first time through. So try not to become discouraged because your final product will show so much growth and character in your writing.

My Reaction to Emily's Response

Emily describes several ways that she has improved her writing over the years. Similar to Meghan, Emily encourages young writers to employ the rule "Show, don't tell" in their writing. (This is an interesting correspondence, because Meghan and Emily don't go to the same school, and don't know each other.) But since we're on the subject, I'll take this opportunity to emphasize this important rule in writing: *Show, don't tell*. It's challenging to learn and to use, but it will *definitely* improve your writing. And you'll be learning about it shortly.

Emily also advises young writers to stop comparing their writing (and their writing methods) to others. Humans are social animals, and it can be difficult being an "independent" writer in school, but this is very good advice. When you compare yourself to others, it often indicates a doubt in your own abilities, and a questioning of your own skill. This is not a bad thing, and it is to be expected among fledgling writers. However, when you have your own original ideas, I encourage you to put on "blinders," stick to your unique perspective, and *write your ideas*. You will have more fun, and your writing will be much more original, lively, and interesting. So, when you receive a new writing assignment, first work to understand what it's asking you to do, and then approach it with confidence and originality.

Emily then encourages young writers to *plan their projects* before they start them, and to *make an outline*. This is terrific advice, and I encourage everyone reading this book to make outlines for all your writing projects, and to use the five-part model that I taught you. However, Emily then says something very insightful. She states that, as you write your paper, it may "take a different shape," and evolve into a better paper than the one you had planned. She is absolutely right about this, and I describe this occurrence as the paper taking an "unexpected turn."

When this happens, always listen to what the paper is urging, and follow the paper's organic energy. *This is where you will do your best writing*. Remember, the five-part outline is an organizing tool, not a dictator made of steel and concrete. Your outline is not written in stone, and it can (and should) change, develop, and evolve as you write your paper. So, don't be afraid to alter your original plan. When your paper tells you it wants to make an unexpected turn, listen to it, and follow where it takes you. If you don't follow the paper's original energy, your writing will be flat and dull. At the same time, however, you must also adhere to the assignment description, and not be pulled completely off course.

Emily closes by telling young writers to "know their audience," which in this case is the teacher. Remember, you are writing a formal academic paper for your teacher, so the paper must be organized, must address the question being asked, and must be written in a formal writer's voice. Finally, she reminds all of you that learning to write is a process of growth and development, so you must stick with it and not get discouraged when things get difficult. This is excellent advice, and I encourage all of you to follow it. I also encourage all of you to *trust the process* and *believe in yourself*, because we're all on an individual journey, unique in all the world.

Jenny (Tenth Grade)

The successes I have had with writing are related to how I have grown as a writer. When I first started out writing, I often dumped my unfiltered thoughts relating to the prompt on paper. I thought revision was just editing, spelling, and grammar issues. Over time I learned about structure, and that a greater length does not always equal greater quality. It is okay to write a shorter response if it means you more effectively get your point across.

When I was younger, I tended to overopinionate informative essays. In order to avoid this, other than just avoiding possessive pronouns, I thought about it like mimicking a news article style. Often, if you are lost on what style you should use, find a piece of text that relates to the prompt you are given and mimic that style. It can be difficult for young writers to simply transition from rambling on a page to a formal, professional tone without something to guide them.

When I'm writing a paper, I use graphic organizers to help organize my thoughts, and this really helps the structure of my writing. These are simple visual tables or charts for the purpose of separating and structuring information. For instance, you might be writing an essay divided into thesis, body paragraphs, and conclusion. For the body paragraphs, you write your topic sentence and find evidence in the text to support your claim so that you don't have to do it later. This sort of planning helps to ensure your essay has all necessary parts and is structured effectively.

Perhaps the biggest enemy to a writer is yourself. I have struggled with self-doubt, I tend to be overly critical of my writing
in early stages, and it leads to giving up. My greatest success is
overcoming this. Sometimes the writing process can be long and
difficult, but your dedication will push out a wonderful product.
Everybody has written at least one good thing in their life, so
when you are telling yourself your writing is trash, remember the
good stuff you have written.

Also, do not be afraid to ask a teacher for help. This can be
especially helpful when you are in a slump of self-doubt, they will
set you on the right track. There is no shame in asking for help.
These have been some things I have learned about writing over
time and hopefully other high school writers can use these as well.

My Reaction to Jenny's Response

In looking back over her writing, Jenny can see where she has
grown, and understands the things that have helped her. Although
she doesn't mention the word "revision," she is starting to understand the purpose of *revising and editing*. She also realizes that
writing "more" does not necessarily make a paper better. Adding
material for the sake of *length* is a common misconception among
fledgling writers that often results in an unfocused paper (full of
unrelated "fluff") that needs to be revised and shortened.

Jenny also learned about being more *objective* in her academic
writing. Being "objective" means writing from a *factual* perspective, rather than including your own feelings and views. In the
past, she would include her own opinions. When writers do this,
they use phrases such as "I believe," "I think," and "I feel." It's
usually best to omit these from formal scholarly writing.

Jenny encourages young writers to learn from authors, perhaps mimicking a "news article" style. This is a very perceptive
insight on her part. Let's say that a newscaster is reporting on a
house fire. You will *never* hear the newscaster say, "I feel so sad
that the house burned down, but I'm glad everyone got out alive."

Rather than saying that, a newscaster will have a more *objective* tone, stating something like, "On Main Street last night, a house burned to the ground. There were no casualties."

Jenny also finds that graphic organizers help her to organize her thoughts and her paper. This sort of preparation is very helpful when you're in the planning stages of writing a paper, especially if you're a visual learner. However, I strongly urge you to follow the five-part essay format I showed you in this book. It performs the functions of a graphic organizer, but more closely replicates the structure of the paper you will write. When you complete a detailed outline, it's fairly simple to convert that into a first draft.

Jenny ends with some positive practical advice for young writers. *Believe in yourself, and banish the thoughts of self-doubt when they happen. Try hard at your writing, and don't give up. Think about your best (or favorite) writing, and don't be afraid to ask your teacher for help.* This is all very good advice.

Meghan (Twelfth Grade)
The most recent thing I'm proud of writing is my college essay. I romanticized everyday people and gave my observations of others. I started by putting people into roles and separating them, then I made the connection of how we are all simultaneously the same and different. I wrote a bit artistically to help "show" and not "tell."

Showing rather than telling can make most if not all your writing pieces more sophisticated. When you show how something proves a certain point, you are feeding your audience examples and proof. An approach of mostly telling can appear like you are barely scraping up enough information. When you show a certain idea, stating the meaning or conclusion of your piece is almost unnecessary. You are letting your audience feel your point. You have the power to ease your readers into a narrative. Although intentional, it's not forced.

Another helpful tool is to give your reader something refreshing. Even for yourself. Try to find a new perspective that made you think. Your reader will be much more invested because it's different. And maybe you won't be so bored because you will be thinking deeper. Something new and refreshing shows your ability to think and comprehend deeply, which is likely to receive a higher grade if you hit all the marks on the rubric. It's also training your mind to think outside of the box for future assignments.

My Reaction to Meghan's Response

Meghan makes two very effective points here. First, she describes one of the most important (and well-known) rules in the kingdom of good writing: *show, don't tell* (Emily discussed this earlier). This is excellent advice, and I encourage all of you to practice it and use it (and it works particularly well when you're writing fiction, such as short stories). But what exactly does "show, don't tell" mean? It's an important question, and I want you to understand the answer.

Show, don't tell means that you should *show* your readers what you're writing about, rather than simply *telling* them. As you write, try to create a picture in readers' minds, so that they can imagine what you're writing about, like viewing a movie in their minds. Here are three examples of *telling* (which is a little bland) versus *showing* (which is very effective). I start with a simple example, then I get a bit longer and more interesting.

Telling: Bob was very tall.

Showing: Bob is the center on our school's basketball team, and he has to duck when he walks through doorways.

Telling: It was extremely cold outside.

Showing: I had never seen the lake frozen so solid. The silver surface was beautiful in the moonlight, and I thought about driving my truck on the ice, to the other side of the lake.

Telling: Samuel was big and strong, and a nice guy.

Showing: Samuel was the strongest and gentlest person I have ever met. His muscles rippled as he walked (it was amazing to see), and all his shirts had to be custom made. But his biggest passion in life was muscle *cars.* I once saw him pick up the engine to a '68 Firebird, and carry it across his garage. It was like he was carrying an empty water bottle. He was smiling the whole time, and talking to me about the '70 Chevelle he just bought.

See how that works? *Showing* rather than *telling* is a very effective way to make your writing powerful and memorable. It will also allow you to develop your ideas more fully, and will add greater meaning to your writing. Read the three examples above slowly and carefully (read them three times each), until you really understand the concept. And read them again tomorrow, because this is really important for your writing. As you write, always try to *show* rather than *tell.* Having said that, I want you to understand that this is a difficult concept to learn and to use. You will *always* have to work at this, but it will improve your writing tremendously.

Meghan's other major point is to make your writing distinctive by giving your readers something "new and refreshing." This is also very effective, and writing teachers refer to this as *taking a risk.* As you write, always try to be original; it will make you and your writing more interesting. No one sees the world exactly as you see it, so stop worrying about what your teacher wants, and tell us how *you* see the issues being discussed. But proceed with caution also. You can be expressive and creative in your scholastic writing, but you have to stick to the assignment description and write within those parameters. After all, there's a grade attached to your paper.

WRITING LESSONS
Learn How to Write a Research Paper

As a high school student, you've probably written papers that included research. If you haven't done this yet, you will. Most students find this challenging, and this is because they haven't been taught how to do it. They haven't been taught about the nature and purpose of research essays, or how to properly include research in them (and there *is* a right way to do it). In this section, I'm going to teach you the basics of writing research essays and how to properly include research in them. It's not as difficult as it sounds, and I'm going to break it down step by step.

First, what is a research essay? In chapter 3, I told you that there are five different types of writing assignments given to students, and this is true. Here they are once again:

1. The Personal Narrative

2. The Informative Essay

3. The Analytical or Interpretive Essay

4. The Academic Argument

5. Creative Writing

Notice that there is no "research essay" among the five. This is because *research* is not its own category. It's a *condition*. You can include research or not. The second, third, and fourth essays on the list can be written with *no* research, or they can be written *with* research. When writing those three types of projects, your teacher may instruct you to write from your thoughts, memories, and feelings, with no research required. This is called an *essay*. Or, your teacher may require that you include research. This is called a *research essay*.

Why do we perform research, and include it in our essays? We perform research for two reasons. First, *we do it to learn about something.* Let's say your teacher wants you to write a paper about the *deforestation of the Amazon rainforest.* (Before we go any further, let me orient you with two simple definitions: The *Amazon rainforest* is an enormous rainforest in South America, and it's quite important to the health of the earth. The term *deforestation* refers to the process of clearing a forest—of plants, animals, and trees—until it is as flat and barren as a vacant lot.) Let's face it: you're probably not an expert on the Amazon rainforest *or* deforestation, and you don't know much about this subject. So, *what would you do? How would you learn about this topic?* You would learn about it by performing research.

The other reason we do research is to *strengthen the points we make in our papers.* Listen carefully, because I really want you to understand this. Let's say that you're writing an essay that includes *no research.* In your essay, you argue passionately that the Amazon rainforest is important and should be preserved. You have just expressed an *opinion* (a personally held belief). It's a *valid* opinion, but it's still an opinion, and opinions are not scientific, and can be easily disproved.

However, let's say you decide to back up your opinion with *research*, in order to make it stronger. What do you do? You can quote well-known experts in the field, perhaps scientists who have written about the subject and who *agree* with you. Well, *that's* a different story. You have just converted your essay into a research paper. You have also converted your "opinion" into an *authoritative scientific statement* backed by legitimate research, and *that* is a very powerful thing. In fact, it's hard to argue with something like that. Okay, let's recap these two major points: We include research in our writing for *two reasons*: (1) to *learn about a subject*, and (2) to support and reinforce the things we say in our papers.

Let's pause for a moment. Before we proceed, I want you to understand what I'm doing here and how I'm teaching you. To help you learn this topic (writing a research paper), I'm going to discuss an assignment on a very specific subject: *the Amazon rainforest and deforestation.* This paper is an *informative essay.* It is designed to *raise awareness* among readers, and it will include research. But there's something a bit different about this paper, so listen carefully.

Although it's not an argumentative paper, I want the writer to take a stance and to present a certain *point of view* to the reader. This is a *type* of informative paper, and we can call it a *persuasive research essay.* Done well, it is a powerful piece of writing that can change readers' minds about a certain topic. Through composing this paper, the writer will raise readers' awareness of the *destructive effects of cutting down the Amazon rainforest* and then turning the land into farms. For this paper, the assignment description would sound something like this:

> *Write an informative paper about the Amazon rainforest and the deforestation that is occurring there. As you write, keep in mind the purpose of this paper. You will raise awareness in readers' minds about the Amazon rainforest and the process of deforestation. You will also inform readers of the destructive effects that deforestation is having on the Amazon rainforest, and (if it continues) how it will negatively impact the rest of the world.*

Now, let's say you have been given a paper on this topic. You have read the assignment description, and you are beginning to plan how you will write this paper. To help you with this process, let's do an exercise right now. So, get a pencil and paper, get comfortable, and perform *five tasks.* Here they are:

1. Read the assignment description carefully. When you understand the assignment deeply, describe it in one single simple sentence. Write it down.

2. Look at the simple sentence, and write down the *essential question* it's asking.

3. Look at the simple sentence and the essential question, and write down a tentative *thesis statement* (it may change as you write your paper).

4. Look at the simple sentence, the essential question, and the thesis statement, and write down *three subtopics*.

5. Look at the simple sentence, the essential question, the thesis statement, the three subtopics, and write down a *working title*.

Take your time, and do your best with these five tasks. This is an important exercise, because when you close this book, you'll be on your own and flying solo.

You can do it, my friend. You can do it. *Single simple sentence . . . Essential question . . . thesis statement . . . three subtopics . . . working title . . .*

Did you finish? Were you able to complete all five tasks? Are you happy with your ideas? I hope so. Here are *my* five responses, offered to you as a guide and a model:

1. The deforestation of the Amazon rainforest is very destructive and will negatively impact the entire earth.

2. *Essential Question:* How is deforestation destructive to the Amazon rainforest, and (if it continues) how will it negatively impact the rest of the earth?

3. *Thesis Statement:* Deforestation is destructive to the Amazon rainforest, and, if it continues, it will also damage the rest of the earth.

4. *Three Subtopics:*

    a. The Amazon rainforest

    b. Deforestation

    c. The Amazon rainforest and the deforestation occurring there

5. *Working Title:* The Amazon Rainforest: A Vanishing Treasure That Must Be Preserved

And now, it's time for another exercise. Pick up your paper and pencil once again, look at the five things you wrote, and convert them into a simple and basic five-part outline. Again, take your time.

Here is mine, offered as a model and a guide:

Working Title: The Amazon Rainforest: A Vanishing Treasure That Must Be Preserved

1. *Introduction* (Your *thesis statement* is the first sentence: Deforestation is destructive to the Amazon rainforest, and, if it continues, it will also damage the rest of the earth.)

2. *First Subtopic:* The Amazon rainforest

3. *Second Subtopic:* Deforestation

4. *Third Subtopic:* The Amazon rainforest and the deforestation occurring there

5. Conclusion

Please read that outline carefully. It is simple, clear, and makes sense. There is nothing fancy or complicated about it, and it sticks to the assignment description and its essential question. It's a very good guide to start organizing and writing an assignment like this.

And now, it's time to perform research. Performing (and using) research for a project is not terribly complicated, but it does take some practice. In this section, I will give you an overview of the process, and I will tell you in detail how to incorporate research into the papers you write in school. Let's start with some guidelines.

As you write your research projects, you will include a mixture of your own words with the research of other writers. Because you're a fledgling writer, your own original writing should be at least 50 percent of the paper (but 75 percent original writing is a good goal to aim for). This means that your *research* should be *less than* 50 percent of the paper (and possibly 25 percent or less). When I write books that include research, I want my own voice to be well over 90 percent of the words in the book. I'm very proud of the books I write, and I feel a true sense of ownership.

For this reason, your paper will *not* be a collection of quotations assembled like a jigsaw puzzle, one quote after another. No. If you do this, you will be the *assembler* of the project, and not the author. Your paper will be written by a bunch of writers whom you have never met, and *you won't be proud of it*. Wait, I know what you're thinking: *I don't know anything about this subject! How can I possibly write about it?* The answer is *research*. Fear not; I will teach you how to do this. If you follow my directions and practice what I teach, you will learn the process of writing a research paper (and possibly impress your teacher as well).

Now, let's say that your teacher wants you to include three resources: *one book and two scholarly articles.* To get the book, go to your school library, and ask the librarian to help you find a book that works for this paper. To get the articles, *do not do an open internet search.* An open search like this will return too many unreliable sources, and your teacher won't like this, and probably won't allow it. Go to your school library once again, and ask your librarian for help. The librarian will show you the library's databases and how to find relevant articles there. Databases are your *best* source of scholarly articles, and they are extremely reliable. If your school library does not have databases, try your local public library, because they will.

When you locate your three sources, I suggest making your bibliography immediately. Please understand that any time you use outside sources, you need a bibliography. This is a page that lists all your sources, and it will usually be the last page in your project. Creating a bibliography is not a creative act, but it is necessary. If you're not sure how to make a bibliography, ask your librarian or your teacher.

And now, it's time to *read your sources*. Read to get a basic understanding of your subject, and *read through the lens of your thesis statement*. When you read for school, *always read with a pencil in your hand*, and annotate as you read. ("Annotating" means writing helpful notes in the margin.) As you read, also look for helpful quotations you can use in your paper, and circle them when you find them. This is very important, so I want to emphasize it:

As you read, look for (and circle) quotes to bring into your paper.
As you read, look for (and circle) quotes to bring into your paper.
As you read, look for (and circle) quotes to bring into your paper.

Look for three good quotes in each source. When you find a good quote, circle it, because these quotes will become the backbone of your paper.

Make sure the quotes you find are useful, but not too long. Your quotes should be about a sentence or two long. In the text of your paper (remember, make it Times New Roman, twelve-point font, double-spaced), your quotes should be about two or three lines long. If a quote is four or more lines in your paper, try to make it shorter (unless you absolutely need the entire thing).

Some students will use several long quotes to gobble up space in the paper, but don't do this. Your teachers are very sharp, and they know all the tricks. If you write in fourteen-point font (much too big) and have quotes half-a-page long (much too long), your teacher will roll their eyes, get a cup of tea, and then write something like this on your essay: *Your paper is too short. Write in twelve-point font, make your quotes three lines each at most, and write another two pages. Revise it, and get it to me by Monday.* And there goes your weekend.

At this point, let's say we have located our three sources (these are all fictional, made up by me):

Book: *The Amazon Rainforest,* by Charlotte Beaumont

Article: "What Is Deforestation?" by Marco Medina

Article: "Saving What's Left of the Amazon Rainforest" (no author given)

We have read our sources, flagged three good quotes in each, and we're getting ready to start writing. Before we start, I need to remind you about something crucial to your success as a student. Do you remember what *plagiarism* is? It's important, and I really want you to understand the concept, because most students don't.

Plagiarism happens when you include the words or ideas of other authors in your paper, but *don't give them credit.* As a writer, you must *always* give authors credit (and it's very easy to do). This is extremely important. At its best, plagiarism is a form of laziness. At its worst, plagiarism is a form of theft. Now, please play attention, because this is a serious subject:

You must *always* give credit to the authors you use in your papers.
You must *always* give credit to the authors you use in your papers.

You must always *give credit to the authors you use in your papers.*

If you don't give them credit, it's plagiarism, *whether you meant to do it, or not.* Plagiarism is always the wrong thing to do, and it will damage your reputation. Now listen carefully: You must always give authors credit whether you *quote them directly* or if you *paraphrase* them. ("Paraphrase" means put their quotes into your own words. When paraphrasing, you do *not* need quotation marks.) Pay attention: If you *paraphrase* authors, you must give them credit.

High school students have a tough time understanding this, so let me say it again: *When you paraphrase a quote (put it into your own words), you must still give the author credit.* (Read that sentence again, and make sure you understand it.) And how do you give authors credit? You do this by giving them a *citation.* And what is a citation? It's a few words (in parentheses) that tell the reader where the information (the quote or paraphrase) came from. This is *easy*, and I'm about to teach you how to do it.

If your quote came from a book, you will provide the last name of the author and the page number where the quote is located. For example, if your quote (or paraphrase) came from Charlotte Beaumont's book on page seventy-two, your citation will go after the quote (or paraphrase), and it will look like this: (Beaumont 72). Don't overthink this. It's *easy.*

Now, let's say your next quote came from Medina's article, but the article didn't have page numbers. (This is very common when doing research on the internet. Many articles don't have page numbers.) In that case, your citation will come after the quote (or paraphrase), and it will include the author's last name only, like this: (Medina). Let's say your next quote came from the article "Saving What's Left of the Amazon Rainforest." For this article, there are no page numbers, and no author is given. (This is fairly common on the internet.) In a case like this, you will provide the *title* of the article only. Your citation will come after the quote (or paraphrase), and it will look like this: ("Saving What's Left of the Amazon Rainforest").

Because you are using these quotes (or paraphrases) *in the text* of your paper, they are called "in-text citations." And this is how these in-text citations will look in your paper:

Quote from a book: "The Amazon rainforest is often called the lungs of the world" (Beaumont 72).

Quote from an article with no page numbers: "Deforestation is terrible for the environment, and has made some animals go extinct" (Medina).

Paraphrase from an article with no author or page numbers: Deforestation has had a tremendous impact on the Amazon rainforest ("Saving What's Left of the Amazon Rainforest").

And now, I want to teach you how to properly use quotes in all your papers. (When I use the term "quotes," I am referring also to paraphrases.) Take a break before we start, and get a cup of coffee or tea. This is important. You have never been taught this, and you never *will* be taught this in the way that I am about to teach it to you. Here we go.

When you find a quote to use in your paper, your goal is to incorporate it seamlessly into your writing so that it contributes to the conversation while also blending in. As you insert each quote, make sure you place it in its correct location, so that it follows the plan of organization you created in your outline. Make sure that your quote is not jarring to the reader. The quote should contribute to the knowledge contained in the paper, and should also flow smoothly. You can't just stick a quote into a paper anywhere you want. Place it where it belongs.

Now, I want you to understand that the quote has to be properly developed and handled. You must talk about the quote, and you must include *your own original words* in the discussion. The quotes are where *your original writing will show up in your paper.* And now, I'll show you how it's done. This is *extremely valuable learning*, so I want you to read this section over and over, and to practice it until you know it.

There are *five steps* to using quotes in the research papers you write for school. Here is a list of the steps:

1. Introduce the quote.

2. Give the quote.

3. Give a citation after the quote.

4. Explain the quote.

5. Interpret the quote.

Those are the five steps. And now, I will explain each one in detail.

1. Introduce the quote. Before providing the quote, always *put some of your own words in front of it.* Keep the introduction simple. Before giving the quote, you might say something like this:

Beaumont states . . .

However, we also have to realize that . . .

Adebayo notices something similar, stating, . . .

Now, let's say that we're going to use the quote from Beaumont's book: "The Amazon rainforest is often called the lungs of the world" (Beaumont 72). You might introduce the quote like this:

This is very important, because . . .

2. Give the quote. After introducing the quote, *give the quote verbatim.* If you are quoting directly, you must include the quote *word for word,* as it's printed in your book or article. You must also put the quote in "quotation marks." If you are *paraphrasing* (putting the quote into your own words), you do *not* need quotation marks. This is because it's not a quote; it's a paraphrase. (But remember: *when paraphrasing, you still need a citation.*) Here is the quote and its introduction:

> This is very important, because "The Amazon rainforest is often called the lungs of the world."

3. Give a *citation* after the quote. We discussed citations above: After using a quote or paraphrase, *tell the reader which source the quote came from.* This is an in-text citation, and you need to do this with quotes and paraphrases. Here is the *introduction, quote,* and *citation*:

> This is very important, because "The Amazon rainforest is often called the lungs of the world" (Beaumont 72).

At this point, I want you to take a breath, and look closely at the quote above. Point to each of the three elements (yes, with your index finger), and see how they look on the page: *introduce the quote (in your own words); give the quote; give the citation.*

4. Explain the quote. Here, you will *explain the quote in your own words.* (If you paraphrase, you probably won't have to provide a second explanation.) *What does the quote mean? What is the writer saying?* Don't assume that your reader understands the quote, so translate it into your own words, and *keep your explanation simple.* And now, pay attention, because I want to tell you something important: In this step (the explanation), *you will generate original writing for your project.* This is one place where you will show up as a writer. Here is the *introduction, quote, citation,* and *explanation*:

This is very important, because "The Amazon rainforest is often called the lungs of the world" (Beaumont 72). This means that the Amazon rainforest produces so much oxygen that it actually helps the rest of the world.

5. Interpret the quote. In this final step, you will *interpret* the quote, relate it to your thesis, and draw conclusions. This is the only part of the process that's a little challenging. However, it's not as difficult as it sounds. Please note that steps four and five (explain the quote and interpret the quote) are a bit like the *summary and commentary* discussed in chapter 4 of this book (so these steps may feel a bit familiar to you).

Interpreting the quote is very important to your writing. This is where you will show up as an original thinker and writer. Practice this process; it's the best way to make your papers your own—and this will give you a great sense of pride. This does take some practice, but *you can do it.* It will expand your thinking and help you grow tremendously as a writer. To interpret the quote, read it carefully, think about it, and ask yourself questions. *What is it saying? What does it mean? What does it suggest? How can I relate this quote to the rest of my paper? How does this quote connect to my thesis statement?* Don't be afraid to take notes and brainstorm on paper.

As you write your interpretation (and connect the quote to your thesis), try to make your interpretation at *least as long as the quote.* Ideally, your interpretation will be *longer* than the quote, because it should discuss larger ideas related to your thesis. Let me give you an example of what I mean. Look at the quote. Notice that it uses a *metaphor*: It calls the Amazon rainforest the "lungs" of the world. It's an interesting statement, and full of meaning.

And now ask yourself some simple questions: *What is the quote suggesting? What are lungs? What do lungs do? Can we live without lungs? Why does the earth need lungs?* And now, let's do an exercise in interpretation. Take your pencil and a sheet of lined paper, and write a short paragraph that interprets Beaumont's quote. Try to make it about three to five sentences long. Take your time. I'll be here waiting for you.

Okay, how did you do? This was your first experience interpreting a quote. If you found it challenging, that's to be expected. It's a new skill to learn and master. It's supposed to be challenging, and you will get better with practice. Here is my interpretation of the quote, offered as a model and a guide:

But why does Beaumont call the Amazon rainforest the "lungs of the world"? What does she mean? Well, trees produce oxygen, and there are lots of trees in the Amazon rainforest. This means that the Amazon rainforest produces lots of oxygen for the world. This is good for all living things, because it helps us to breathe. So, if the Amazon rainforest is the earth's lungs, it's very important. We all need lungs to breathe and to live. Without lungs, we would all die. So, we really need to stop the deforestation in the Amazon rainforest. We need it to breathe and to live.

And now, let's put it all together. Here is a very nice paragraph that contains all five steps of incorporating research into a research paper.

> *This is very important, because "The Amazon rainforest is often called the lungs of the world" (Beaumont 72). This means that the Amazon rainforest produces so much oxygen that it helps the rest of the world. But why does Beaumont call the Amazon rainforest the "lungs of the world"? Well, trees produce oxygen, and there are lots of trees in the Amazon rainforest. This means that the Amazon rainforest produces lots of oxygen for the earth. This is good for all living things, because we need oxygen to breathe. We also need lungs to breathe, and to live. Without lungs, we would die. So, we really need to stop the deforestation in the Amazon rainforest. We need it to breathe and to live.*

And *that's* how to incorporate research (and quotes) into your paper. I have taken a quote and turned it into a strong paragraph. See how that goes? Read it over three times, and read it again five times tomorrow. Each time you read it, I want you to notice *all five steps* in the process: (1) introduce the quote; (2) give the quote; (3) give the citation; (4) explain the quote; (5) interpret the quote. I also want you to note how much original writing is in this paragraph.

I started with a simple quote (it's about one line long), and I turned it into a well-written paragraph that contains *lots of my own original writing*. See how that works? This is how you will bring your own original thoughts and words into your research papers. This is how you will show up as an original writer and thinker. If you do this, your own writer's voice will carry the paper. Your paper will be truly *yours*, and *you will be very proud of it*. Please learn this method, practice it, and use it. It works, and it will change the way you write for school. And now, let's put everything together, and look at a detailed five-part outline of this paper:

Working Title: The Amazon Rainforest: A Vanishing Treasure That Must Be Preserved

1. Introduction (one paragraph; write this last)

   a. Thesis statement: Deforestation is destructive to the Amazon rainforest, and, if it continues, it will also damage the rest of the earth.

   b. Briefly discuss what this paper is about, along with *your point of view*.

   c. Briefly discuss why this subject is important.

2. First subtopic: The Amazon rainforest

   a. Overview of the Amazon rainforest

b. Details about the Amazon rainforest

c. Describe why the Amazon rainforest is so important

3. Second subtopic: Deforestation

a. What is deforestation? (define and discuss)

b. Why is it happening? (causes)

c. How is it damaging to environments? (results)

4. Third subtopic: How the Amazon rainforest has been damaged by deforestation

a. Describe how it's been damaged by deforestation.

b. Describe some ways to help the Amazon rainforest to *heal*.

c. Describe some ways to *prevent* (or *reduce*) the deforestation occurring there.

5. Conclusion (one paragraph)

a. Restate your main points (some summary here).

b. Discuss what might happen if we lose the Amazon rainforest.

c. End on a note of *hope*. Is this situation getting any better? Why should we remain hopeful about the existence of the Amazon rainforest? Is there something the "average" person can do to help this situation?

Read that outline slowly and carefully three times today, and another three times tomorrow. Note its simplicity and its deep sense of organization. There is nothing fancy in that outline. I discussed the topic in terms that make sense, and it flows smoothly (and logically) from one idea to another. Learn how to make outlines like this, and let them guide your writing. You will never again say, "I don't know what to write."

In this book, I have given you several detailed outlines for different types of papers. Please look at all of them carefully, see how they are constructed and organized. Also, make sure you practice the method I taught you to incorporate research (the quotes you use) into the papers you write for school. And then, bring this new knowledge into your writing for school, and use it in all your papers.

And now, let's turn to the final chapter in this book. It's time to get *creative*.

CHAPTER 6

Teens Learn

Creative Writing: Personal Essays and Short Stories

LET'S GET CREATIVE

In this chapter, I'm going to do something different, something I have never done before in any of my books. Among nearly all the high school students who assisted me with this volume, there was a powerful cry for *creativity*. As a former English teacher, this did not surprise me. Young people love to be creative; they love to write about their own lives, and they love to express themselves through writing freely. So, that's what we'll be doing here. We're going to get creative. But it's going to be a little different—for me, for you, and for writer's guides in general.

In this chapter, I'm going to teach you two different types of creative writing. We'll start with the *personal essay*, and we'll conclude with the *short story*. This gives us a nice balance of non-fiction and fiction. Both types are very creative, and I encourage you to do both after you finish reading this book. In the first part of this chapter, I will show you how to write an *essay* based on some aspect of your life. In the latter half, I will teach you how to write a short story.

But here's the unusual part of this chapter. After I teach you how to write a personal essay, I'm going to share with you one of *my own personal essays.* This will be an example for you to follow. It's a very strong essay, and you'll enjoy reading it. Then, after I teach you how to write a short story, I'm going to share with you one of my own short stories. It's a good story, and you'll like it. And it's about a young person named Danny. And Danny is *me.* Let's get started.

Learn How to Write a Personal Essay

What is a personal essay? It is an essay written about some aspect of your personal life, so it does *not* need research. It's about something that really happened, so it's a form of *nonfiction.* But it's not a simple retelling of an event in your life. If you write about "the time you won the big game," that's cute, but what's the payoff for the reader? When you write a personal essay, start by choosing something *meaningful.*

The subject of your essay must be something that means a great deal to you, not just something that you "liked." No one is interested in hearing what you "liked." It must be relevant, for you *and* the reader, and it must have a meaningful *theme.* Here are some themes to consider: *growing up; friends; school; family; pets; moving; parents; siblings; bullying; being different; loneliness; trying hard; working hard, your first job; goals and dreams for the future.* And I'm sure you can come up with others.

As you develop your personal essay, fill your readers' minds with meaning, make us think about something important, share your insights, and *teach us what you learned.* There must be some sort of payoff for the reader. Remember, we read for two reasons only. We read for *enjoyment,* and we read to *learn something.* Try to do both in your personal essays.

To write a personal essay, start with brainstorming possible topics. To do this, it's always helpful to ask yourself questions, and then write down the answers (so that you don't forget them). Here are some good questions to ask yourself:

What was an event in your life that *taught* you something?

What was an event in your life that somehow *changed* you?

What was something *difficult* that helped you to grow?

What is the most difficult thing you have ever done? What did you learn?

Who is (or was) the most influential person in your life? How was he or she influential? What did she do? What did he teach you? Why is this person important to you?

What was something that *frightened* you? Did you stand up to your fear? If not, why not? Tell us about it. What happened? What did you learn?

Tell us about something that you *regret*. What happened? Why do you regret it? What did you learn?

How did a loss eventually become a "gain"?

What was the best moment of your life?

What was the worst moment of your life?

Tell us about a *success* in your life. What happened? What did you learn?

Tell us about a *failure* in your life. What happened? What did you learn?

Was there ever a time that you could have done something positive or helpful, but chose not to? Why did you make this choice? Why did you remain a "bystander"? How do you feel about it? What did you learn?

Is there a time (or event) in your life that you would do differently? Describe it. Why?

Is there a place in your life that is very important to you?
Tell us about it.

Up to this point, I have given you some *themes* to include in
your essay, and some *questions* to get you thinking. When you
have an idea germinating in your fertile mind, I want you to do an
exercise. It's called *freewriting*. You can do it on the computer, or
on lined paper with a pencil, but I prefer pencil and paper. Sometimes the old ways are hard to beat. Here's how it works. Make
sure a clock is visible, and start writing for *five minutes*. Just start
scribbling your thoughts.

The first few times you do this, you can write whatever is in
your mind, and don't worry about grammar or punctuation. Just
write the thoughts flashing in your fruitful mind. (My ninth-grade
teacher did this at the beginning of every class, and I loved it. She
called it *Potpourri*.) When you get a feel for this exercise, do some
freewriting on the *experience* you want to write about, or the *theme*
you want to explore.

As you begin to understand this process, feel free to increase
the time (perhaps up to ten minutes). Always keep your notes, and
read them over to see the insights that showed up and revealed
themselves. You will be very surprised by the things that emerge,
and the insights you "accidentally" reveal on paper. This freewriting exercise is a great way to bring subconscious ideas into your
conscious mind, where they will quietly reveal themselves on
paper.

And now, I'm going to give you the three main ingredients to
writing a personal essay. This is important stuff, so pay attention.
Here they are: (1) *description*, (2) *reflection*, (3) *insight*. You can
remember them by using the acronym DRI (pronounced "dry").
You must include all three in all your personal essays, and here is
each one in detail:

1. *Description*. You will begin your essay by describing what
happened. This must come early in the essay, or the reader will

have no idea what you're talking about. And now, I'm going to give you one of my secrets: don't describe this like you're writing an essay for school—*tell a story*. Use storytelling techniques such as characterization, dialogue, and first-person narration. (A first-person narrator uses the terms "I" and "me.") After all, it's *your* story told from *your* perspective.

Here's another writer's secret: You are not writing "facts," you are writing *truth*. No one expects you to remember every detail from your life several years ago. For example, you can't possibly recall the conversations you had, word-for-word. Tell your story the best way you can, and *shape it to your purposes*. If you don't remember someone's name, *give them a new name*. Your *theme* is more important than factual "accuracy." We read essays like this not to memorize "facts," but to encounter *truths*. As you write your essay, always keep your central theme in mind, and write to produce *meaning*, not to list facts. No one cares about the facts of your life. Give us the *truth* of what you learned and how you grew. Help us to see the world as we've never seen it before.

2. *Reflection*. After describing your situation, it's time to start *reflecting* on it. Think back to the event, and see it clearly in your mind (close your eyes if it will help). Use your memory and engage your senses. *What do you see? What do you hear? What were you feeling when this situation happened? What are your feelings now? Why is this memory important to you? Would you be the same person if this event never happened? How might you be different?*

Explain what this memory means to you, and describe your feelings about it. Tell your readers (and yourself) why this event is noteworthy, and why you're still thinking about it. While all these thoughts and feelings are still pulsing in your mind, get your pencil and lined paper, and do some freewriting for a few minutes. Try to describe and understand how you are truly feeling about this thing, and why it's so important to you. Label these notes "Reflection," and reference them as you write your essay.

3. *Insight.* In this section, you will focus on two major goals. First, describe what the experience *taught you.* Second, suggest what your readers can *learn* from the experience. Don't be too "preachy" here; let your experience and your insights do the talking. Again, take yourself back to the scene, and visualize it happening. *What do you see? What lessons can it teach you? What did you learn from these events?*

Remember, the lessons you discuss should be meaningful and memorable. You can write this section by asking yourself a simple question: *What did I learn from this situation?* And then talk about it, and talk about why it's a valid lesson for you *and* your readers. Once again, get your pencil and lined paper and do some freewriting on the lessons you learned, and how they changed the way you see the world. Label them "Insight," and keep them near as you write your essay.

As you plan your essay, I want you to once again make a five-part outline. This time, the three subtopics will be description; reflection; insight (DRI). To help you get started, here is a simple outline for your personal essay:

1. Introduction (Write this last.)

2. *Description*: What happened? Describe it. Tell a story.

3. *Reflection*: What are your thoughts and feelings about it? Why is it meaningful to you?

4. *Insight*: What did you learn from this event? What can others learn from it?

5. Conclusion (summary; emphasize the points you want readers to remember)

And now, here is my own personal essay. I wrote this a few years ago to see how I felt about something interesting that happened to me a long time ago. I like this essay very much, and it was immediately accepted for publication in a respectable online journal. However, the people at the journal wanted to "edit" my essay, which meant (in this case) removing all its quirks and character and everything that made it special. I respectfully withdrew my submission, which is the only time I ever did that. And now, here is my essay, published for the first time anywhere.

Encounter with Genius

When I got out of the Marines, the first job I got was assistant manager in what was then the largest bookstore on Long Island. It meant a huge cut in pay, but I was really excited. I had always been in love with books, and I had always wanted to be a writer, and my highest dream (after writing a book) was to have a library in the house that I would someday own. I would build the library myself, and it would have curved windows and shelves everywhere, just like a real library. Oh, *yes*. But until that happened, I had the beautiful bookstore.

I loved being around the new books. New books everywhere. The scent of new books and new ink, the shiny new covers, the buzz of something new and special. But my favorite part was meeting authors. We'd have a book-signing every once in a while, and I used to stare at the authors like they were made of miracles. *They did it*, I would think to myself. *Somehow, they actually did it.* I always had them sign a book for me, and I always tried to make small talk so I could reflect back later on our "conversation."

"So, do you have any advice for an aspiring writer?" I used to ask them.

"Get an agent," was the usual response.

I learned quickly that working in a big bookstore was extremely difficult work. *Extreme*ly difficult. I didn't like the mercenary end of things, the obsessive "bottom line" mentality, and every day I went home with swollen feet and hurt feelings from being yelled at by unhappy customers. I stuck with it for two years, and finally I was promoted to manager of a small bookstore in a crowded mall. The small bump in pay was accompanied by a huge bump in responsibility, but I was pretty happy about it. New beginnings are always exciting.

CHAPTER 6

As a shiny new manager, the first thing I had to do was attend the annual manager's conference. This meant a few days in a nice hotel in Baltimore, eating hotel food (which is usually pretty good), and schmoozing with other managers from around the country. The first evening was a mixer. A party of sorts to meet our fellow managers. Being a little shy, I always found these things difficult, and, as a new manager, I didn't know a single person there. And to make it worse, someone high up in the company decided that this should be a costume party.

A *costume* party. An actual *costume* party. I was horrified.

I mean, think about it. Here I was, in a strange hotel, walking into a room full of strangers, dressed as *Indiana Jones*. But I started to circulate and meet my fellow managers, and really it wasn't so bad. They loved my costume, and for the night I was christened "Indy." (And, for the record, any time you can become one of your heroes for a night, that's pretty cool.) I chatted and sipped ginger ale, and someone told me that we were going to have a surprise speaker later that night. An author. *Daniel Boorstin, ever heard of him?* No, but that's awesome, I thought. I'll get a book signed, and ask him if he has any advice for an aspiring writer.

And that's when my night got really good.

I decided at some point to get some fresh air, so I left the party and stood outside the doors of the hotel. It was a beautiful September evening, the world was cooling off, and there I spotted the man who hired me. I'll call him "Bob." He was a company vice president, and he stood talking to a nice-looking couple. They were well dressed, and appeared to be in their seventies. The man wore big glasses and a dark suit with a bow tie, and he carried a large book and a small portfolio. I walked over and greeted them, and Bob shook my hand. "Tim," he said, "this is Daniel Boorstin and Mrs. Boorstin." I shook their hands. *He did it*, I thought to myself, and gazed at Mr. Boorstin as if he were something very special. And I found out later that he was.

"Tim," Bob said, "the Boorstins want to have dinner before Mr. Boorstin speaks later. Would you care to join them?" *Wow*— right place at the right time.

"Yes!" I shouted, and Mr. Boorstin smiled at me and said, "Dinner with Dr. Jones," and we all laughed.

The hotel restaurant was dark and the food was good, and I remember thinking how lucky I was. There were over a hundred managers at the conference, and I was *the only one* having dinner with the guest speaker. I was thrilled, but a little nervous. I began to suspect there was something very unusual about the Boorstins, and I thought maybe I was intruding. But they were very nice, and they put me at ease, and Mr. Boorstin came across as a "regular guy." I could see myself chatting with him over a fence and under a summer sky, asking him if I could borrow his lawn mower, or maybe a hammer. He was that kind of guy. He really was.

We talked a little about books—a thing we all had in common—and they began to ask me questions about *me*. This is my clearest memory of the dinner. It was ironic, really—I wanted to ask Mr. Boorstin *what's it like being*—and *do you have any advice for*—but they seemed fascinated with me, and they peppered me with questions faster than I could answer them. They both did. I looked from one to the other and tried to answer their questions as quickly as I could, and it was like being at a rapid-fire ping pong match.

So Tim, where are you from?
Where did you go to school?
What did you major in?
Did you like being in the military?
Do you read much?
Do you like poetry?
Who are your favorite authors?
What's it like being a bookstore manager?
What's wrong with the education system?

And on, and on, and on. I finally covered my face and shook my head and laughed at the impossible task they had set up for me, and they laughed too.

"Tim," Mrs. Boorstin said, "you really must come visit us. We live in Washington, DC, and we would love to have you stay with us. Really." She wrote their phone number and address on a piece of paper, and handed it to me. "Will you visit us? Please?"

"Yes, I would love to," I said. But I never did visit the Boorstins, and this is one of the great regrets of my life.

At some point during our dinner, I told the Boorstins my dream of having my very own library in my very own house. I didn't own a house yet, but someday I would, and that house would have a library in it. Of that I was sure. And I would build it myself.

"Sounds terrific." Mr. Boorstin nodded. "I'm a big fan of libraries. I was a librarian once in a pretty big library. My friend Louie—he passed away a few years ago—he had a nice library in his house."

"Your friend Louie?" I asked.

"Yes," he said. "He wrote western novels, but he was a great reader too. Most people don't know that." He took a sip of water.

I stared at him. *No. Impossible. It couldn't be.* "Your friend Louie," I said. "He's not . . . he—he isn't—"

"Louis L'Amour," he said. He buttered some bread and took a bite.

I stared at him again and processed this new information. Louis L'Amour was one of my heroes and one of my favorite authors. And still is. He was a truly great writer whose literary abilities have gone largely uncelebrated.

"You knew Louis L'Amour," I said, idiotically.

"Yes, and I wish you could have seen his library," he said. "The guy must have owned, oh, twenty thousand books. He finally had so many that he had to build shelves in front of shelves." Mr. Boorstin laughed and made a swinging gesture with his hands. "The bookcases opened like doors, and there were more books behind them. He was a great reader, and he loved American history. And his books aren't just westerns, you know. They're well-researched historical novels."

I couldn't believe it. I had read Louis L'Amour's novels and his wonderful autobiography *The Education of a Wandering Man*. It was mostly about the extensive (and joyful) reading he did as a young man. L'Amour said that he dropped out of school at age fifteen, but "not out of education." And now I was hearing about it firsthand from someone who actually knew him. I was stunned.

We finished dinner, and Mr. Boorstin looked at his watch. "Well, it's almost that time," he said, and looked at his wife. "Ready?"

"Sure," she said. We paid the bill and stood and she turned to me and smiled. "Tim, you really must come visit us. Please. We'd love to have you over."

I said I would love to, and I thanked them for everything, and we walked to the hotel salon where Mr. Boorstin would give a talk.

His presentation was quite captivating, and he spoke about his new book *The Creators*. This was the big book he was carrying.

This book—a sweeping eight-hundred-page masterwork—explores the creative impulse in humanity through the ages, the genius creators that humanity has produced, and the wonderful things that they have left to the world. The book is huge and marvelous, and I don't know how he did it. After his speech, I waited in line and asked him to sign a copy for me. I look at the book today, and I see that it's gotten a bit dusty. I also see that he inscribed it thusly: *"For Tim Horan—an energetic colleague in the world of books—from Daniel Boorstin."*

***

About ten years ago, I thought of that evening and of Daniel Boorstin, and I had a funny, fleeting thought: *Would he remember me? Would he remember his wife's kind invitation? Was it too late for a visit?* A quick bit of research revealed that, yes, it was too late. He passed away in 2004. He was eighty-nine.

Yes, yes, I thought. Of course it was too late. Of course. Of course. Opportunities such as that . . .

I felt sad and I felt a pang of cold loneliness and I felt I had missed out on something special. I began reading up on the man to try, I suppose, to make up for what I had missed. I read obituaries and biographies, and I was shocked at what I found there. I couldn't believe what I saw, what he had done, who he really was. He was a virtual "who's who" of academia and librarianship and writing, and I had absolutely no idea. Here are some of his accomplishments:

He entered Harvard University at fifteen years old.

He was a *Rhodes Scholar.* He earned two degrees at the University of Oxford (England), and became an English barrister (lawyer).

He earned a Doctorate in Law from Yale and became an attorney.

He was a Harvard professor.

He was a professor at the University of Cambridge (in England).

He was the first Chair in American History at the Sorbonne in France.

He was a history professor at the University of Chicago for twenty-five years (despite having no formal training in history, a fact that amused him).

He wrote over twenty books.

He won the Pulitzer Prize in History for his book *The Americans: The Democratic Experience.*

He was the Director of the National Museum of History and Technology at the Smithsonian Institution.

He was the *Librarian of Congress* from 1975 to 1987.

Did you get that last bit? He was *the* Librarian of Congress for twelve years, nominated by the president of the United States (Gerald Ford). The Library of Congress is *the largest library in the world*, and he was in charge of it.

I was speechless.

Think about those things I listed above. Any *one* of them would constitute the achievement of a lifetime, and Dr. Boorstin did them *all.*

I thought back to the night Indiana Jones had dinner unwittingly with the Pulitzer Prize-winning Librarian of Congress. *Mr. Boorstin, would you please pass the bread sticks?* Had I known who he really was, what would I have done differently? No, it was probably better that I didn't know.

If I could meet with Dr. Boorstin today—and conjure up the visit that I missed—I would tell him that I finally did buy a house, and I built a library in it. I bought a little log cabin on a pretty little lake, and, yes, I built the library myself. Turns out I'm a pretty good carpenter. I would also tell him that I gave up selling books to become a teacher, a librarian, and a writer. I think he would like that. And, over coffee—he would serve it black and steaming and strong—I would ask him the question that I didn't get to ask: "So, do you have any advice for an aspiring writer?"

Having read some of his work, and having read about him, I can take a pretty good guess at his answer. I think he would say this: *Discover your consuming passions, then learn as much as you can about them. Then write about them constantly, and be as honest as you can with your readers.* Yes, I think he would say that, and I suppose this would be good advice for any writer.

And then maybe he would give me a glimpse of his sacred study, and perhaps a backstage tour at the Library of Congress. And wouldn't that be wonderful. Later, back at his house, there would be more coffee, and we would sit and talk about books, and we would talk about reading. But it wouldn't be a pedantic conversation. It would be Ray Bradbury under the covers by flashlight.

The murky jungles and lost civilizations of Edgar Rice Burroughs. The promise of baseball on a Saturday afternoon, with a copy of *Treasure Island* tucked in your back pocket, and a shady tree later. Lemonade maybe. It would be like that.

Looking back on my memories and at what I've written here, I see that this essay is a celebration of the world of books. But I also see it's more than that. It's a reminder to see beyond the surfaces of things, and to recognize and embrace the small miracles that happen to us every once in a while. It is also, I now realize, a look back at a very interesting time in my life when my future was an unwritten volume, chaotic and inchoate, full of longing and mystery and possibility.

I suppose this essay was, at least partly, an attempt to make sense of a wonderful experience, and to extract greater meaning and insight from it. And also, I suppose, to give you the opportunity to do the same. So, I suppose this essay is partly for you, and partly for me. And, in its final edited version, shiny and new, I suppose it is a joyful homage to things that really happened, and a gentle, mournful whisper to things that might have been.

***

That's my essay. I hope you liked it. I'd like you to read it once a day for the next few days. As you read it, try to identify where I include *description*, *reflection*, and *insight*. They're all present, and they're not too hard to spot. As you read, also try to identify the *themes* that I explore in the essay. There are a few, and I mention some of them in the conclusion. However, I don't mention the *central* theme of the essay—what it's really about. I leave that as a mystery for the reader to discover. Can *you* figure it out?

And now, let's write a short story.

Learn How to Write a Short Story

When I teach students how to write a short story, I always start with a simple question: *how many stories are in the world?* After listening to all their questions and guesses and baffled replies, I surprise everyone by saying this: "There is only *one* story in the world." And my students look at me in wonder and wait for me to explain this miracle. And I do.

My claim that there is only *one story* in the world is a teacher tactic designed to raise engagement and to keep my teaching simple and understandable. But it's also largely true. And now, I'm going to tell you why. I'm also going to give you the framework for virtually every story you will ever read, every movie you will ever see, and every story you will ever write. When you learn this basic structure, you will better understand the books you read and the movies you watch. You will also be able to write good short stories. There are two basic versions of story-structure, and here they are:

1. The Problem to Solve. *Every story has a problem for characters to solve.* So, when you read a story or watch a movie, try to identify the problem to solve (because it's definitely there). The character who attempts to solve the problem is usually the protagonist (the main character). If the problem is solved, it's usually a happy ending. If the problem is *not* solved, it's usually an unhappy ending. This is a valid explanation of story-structure, and you may have heard this from some of your teachers.

2. The *One-Story* Approach. Here is the second story-structure. I greatly prefer this method, and consider it a more effective approach than the first one. I use it in my own writing, I teach it to my students, and now I'm teaching it to *you*. I call it the "One-Story" approach, because it can be applied to virtually every story in the world, reducing them all to *one story*. There are three parts to this story-structure: *Grail; Conflict; Resolution.* Here they are in detail:

   a. *Grail.* A character (sometimes multiple characters) wants something very badly, and has a clear goal to achieve (this character is usually the protagonist). The goal must be meaningful and worthy of being pursued.

Attaining the goal will improve the character's life, or improve the lives of others, or (possibly) even improve the world. If the character does not achieve the goal, something very bad will happen (we call this "consequences"). I refer to this goal as the "grail," and I will explain this term shortly.

b. *Conflict.* Someone or something tries to prevent the character from attaining the goal. *What* is the conflict? *Who* is the conflict? Why are they trying to prevent the protagonist from achieving the goal? Perhaps the conflict is not a person, but a natural *event* such as a blizzard or an earthquake or a tsunami (and each of those can ruin your day). How will the protagonist deal with the conflict? What will he or she do? What are the *consequences* of not achieving the goal? As you write your conflict, make it *fierce.* If the goal (or grail) were easy to attain, it would not be worth pursuing (that's a universal law on planet earth).

c. *Resolution.* This is the conclusion to the story. Here, the protagonist either achieves the goal (usually a happy ending) or does *not* achieve the goal (usually an unhappy ending). How does the protagonist achieve the goal? How does the protagonist feel when the goal is achieved? What are the effects of achieving the goal? How does the goal change the protagonist's life? Does it change the lives of others? Does it somehow change (or improve) the world?

And that, my friends, is the structure of every story you will ever read, and all the stories you will ever write. And now, I will tell you why I call the goal the "grail." A thousand years ago (or thereabouts), stories were being written about King Arthur, the legendary king of England. In these stories, King Arthur was obsessed with finding an important religious artifact called the "Holy Grail." So, he sent his knights out on a special mission: *find the Holy Grail*. And now, I will use the One-Story approach to write a very, *very* short story about one of King Arthur's knights, who was named Sir Galahad:

Once upon a time, Sir Galahad learned that the Holy Grail was being kept in a gloomy castle guarded by a fierce fiery dragon. Galahad fought the dragon valiantly and won the fight. Galahad obtained the Grail and brought it back to King Arthur. And they lived happily ever after.

Technically speaking, that's a short story. (We would actually call it a "short short story," or "flash fiction.") Let's break it into its *Grail, Conflict,* and *Resolution*:

1. *Grail:* the actual Holy Grail

2. *Conflict:* the fiery dragon who guards the Grail

3. *Resolution:* Sir Galahad slays the dragon, finds the Grail, and brings it to King Arthur.

If you watch a movie called *Indiana Jones and the Last Crusade* (starring my hero Dr. Indiana Jones), you'll note that the grail of that story is actually the Holy Grail. Those moviemakers certainly knew their business, and gave us a marvelous tale, along with a good-natured wink at those who understand storytelling (and if you haven't seen this movie yet, *see it*. You will *love* it.)

And now, here is another *flash fiction* example made up by me. As you read it, try to spot the grail, conflict, and resolution:

Aliyah and the Mountain

When Aliyah fell off the rock, she heard a *snap* and knew that she had broken her leg. She pushed her face into the dirt and leaves, and screamed with pain—and remembered with horror that she left her cell phone in her car. The mountain was huge, and she wondered how she could make her descent. The sun was setting, and Aliyah understood her situation very clearly: *get off the mountain or die.* Gritting her teeth, she began dragging herself down the mountain, through the forest and rocks and streams that covered it. Fourteen hours later, Aliyah spotted her car in the parking lot, and wept with joy.

Can you spot the grail, conflict, and resolution? Here they are:

1. *Grail:* Get off the mountain and live

2. *Conflict:* A broken leg; a long way down the mountain; the cold and dark of the night

3. *Resolution:* She made it to the parking lot (a comforting sign of civilization), and lived.

And now you know the structure of writing a story. This precious knowledge should assist you greatly as you write your own stories—which I strongly encourage you to do. Try to write one story each month for a year. You'll be surprised at how much you improve as a writer. Here is a simple five-part outline to guide you in writing your stories:

Working Title of Your Story

1. *Introduction:* Provide the setting (time and place), situation, and characters

2. *Grail:* The protagonist's goal

3. *Conflict:* An element trying to prevent the protagonist from reaching the goal. There are serious consequences for not achieving the grail.

4. *Resolution:* The protagonist achieves the grail (or doesn't).

5. *Conclusion:* What happens as a result of the Resolution?

And now, I want to share with you one of my own short stories. I really like this one, and I think you'll like it too. Like my personal essay above, here it is, published for the first time anywhere.

A Sad Sort of Laughter

When I was very young, my father seemed a giant of a man and I was very frightened of him. I loved him, but he scared me just the same, and to be safe I took everything he said to me as an order. His direct orders were easy. I did what he said and that was that and he didn't get angry or unhappy. His indirect orders were more difficult, but this was something I had to learn. There was what he *said*, and there was what he *wanted*, and I had to figure out which to do.

If he gave you a choice and you chose the right one he would never say anything, but would smile just a little and there would be a gentleness in the way he looked at you or spoke to you, in the angle of his jaw and the set of his shoulders. But if you chose the wrong one a dark disapproval would fall from his eyes and it was very difficult to bear because he was unhappy, and I wanted to make him happy and be the boy he wanted me to be. And also, I now confess, there was that part of me, hidden and secret, that said *yes* to his wishes and didn't want to miss anything because maybe the old man was right about things.

He beat me once when I was very small, and this too was secret. I was nine years old and I came home from school one day with bits of blood on my upper lip and when my father saw me I remember looking down and waiting for him to say something. The clock ticked very loudly in the kitchen and I could feel the disapproval from his eyes falling on me. My mother saw me and she said, "*Oh* God," and quickly called the school.

My father said, "Danny, come here," and so I went into the living room and he sat in his armchair and turned on the light and pulled me close to him. His breath was sweet and heavy and his hands felt rough and reassuring on my face, and his eyes squinted as he looked at my face. I suddenly felt very safe and very sleepy and I wanted to put my head on his chest and fall asleep in his arms. He ran his fingertips over my nose and over the dried blood under my nose and he asked me if it hurt, and I said it did hurt a little.

"Was he bigger than you?" he asked me.

"Yes," I said.

"What was it about?"

"Nothing," I said, and looked down and waited for the question I knew he would ask.

"Did you fight back?"

I remember looking at the floor again and wanting to be the boy he wanted me to be and trying hard not to cry in front of him because I knew I had to cry sometime about this.

"Did you fight back?"

At that moment I hated the question and I hated him for asking it and I think I would have liked for him to hit me or hug me and tell me it would be alright, that he would take care of everything. But I also knew that wouldn't happen.

"Danny," he said, "did you fight back?"

"No, Papa," I whispered back to him, "I didn't."

That was the answer he expected but he had to ask it anyway and so he sat back and nodded just a little and I knew I had to stand there a while longer and wonder how this would all turn out and I still had tomorrow's bus ride to worry about, and the day after that, and the day after that.

But then my father did something that surprised me (and to this day surprises me)—he put his hands on my shoulders and hugged me and I nearly cried with the unexpected joy of it. I think sometimes it was the only thing he ever did that was pure and right and true. Then he looked in my eyes and told me that the same thing happened to him once when he was about my age. It had never occurred to me that my father could be bullied by anyone, and so I asked him what did you do.

He sat back and smiled. "I made the mistake of telling your grandfather—God rest his soul—that I lost the fight. And Danny, the *beating* he gave *me*"—here my father sat back and closed his eyes and shook his head slowly—"and he told me it would happen every day until I won the fight."

"What did you do?" I asked.

My father laughed just a little. "I can tell you, Danny, your grandfather hit harder than that boy—so the very next day, I found him—Ray Conklin was his name—and I walked up to him and punched him in the nose just as hard as I could. Blood everywhere, and he fell down and he never bothered me after that. Yes," he shook his head again, "he was something, your grandfather. Boy, oh *boy.*"

I looked down again because I knew I could never do that and my father seemed to know what I was thinking because he just said, "Danny, you *have* to," and then he walked away and told my mother that it would be alright.

The next day I came home with blood under my nose again and the world looked funny to me because one of my eyes was beginning to swell shut, so I sat down on the curb in front of my house and cried for a while because I didn't want to face my father like that. I knew the questions he would ask and just as I was wiping my eyes dry and breathing more smoothly, I heard the front door open behind me and my father said, "Danny, come in here."

My father knelt in front of me in the kitchen and looked closely at my nose and my lip and my eye and he said, "Did you hit him back?" I looked down at the floor and said, "No, Papa, I couldn't," and my father nodded and walked from the room and said, "Danny, get changed and meet me in the backyard in five minutes."

I pulled on a white tee shirt very slowly because my face was beginning to swell and it hurt badly and I remember that everything seemed strange because I was frightened to meet my father in the backyard, and also frightened *not* to meet him there.

When I saw my father in the backyard he had on a pair of boxing gloves (old, reddish things he said belonged to *his* father) and he was slapping them together. There were another pair on the ground and he kicked them toward me and said, "Get them on," and then he said, "we'll do this every day until you can hit him back." When I had the gloves on my father knelt in the grass and said, "Walk towards me, and hold your hands like this. No," he said, "like *this*; higher, protect your face," and when I was close, he slashed a punch straight into my swollen eye. I remember screaming and I fell on the ground and pulled at the gloves with my teeth and threw my arms over my face and sobbed when he stood over me. I wanted to believe that it was an accident, that he hadn't meant to hit me in an eye already dark with pain and shame and fear. And I saw in his eyes that he wasn't enjoying it when he said, "Danny, put your gloves back on and stand up." And when I didn't do it he said, "Get up, he'll be there tomorrow."

When I worked the gloves back on and stood in front of my father I was still sobbing, holding my gloves up and blinking my eyes and breathing in short, quick gasps and not caring if my father saw my tears. But now, looking back, I think my sobbing was not so much from the throbbing I felt in my eye as from the sense that my dad had just betrayed me.

"Okay, Danny," he said, "walk toward me, and hold your hands like this," and I walked toward him and protected my hurt eye. When I got close, I threw a gentle jab toward his chin and he landed a quick solid punch on my nose. I screamed again with the pain and the stinging raw shock of it and I staggered back, and I remember thinking *this time that it was no accident.* My father was deliberately hurting me.

I pushed a glove across my nose and saw tears and streaks of bright red blood on it, and when I showed him my glove and told him I was bleeding and that it hurt, he said again, "Hold your hands like this—up high—and walk toward me," and I felt a fury inside me and a red raging hatred and I ran at him trying with all my strength to hurt him and kill him. And as I threw punch after punch, I grunted and panted and sobbed, and he just whispered, "Punch straighter, hit harder," and when I finally landed a straight, solid punch on the side of his jaw, he stood up and I wondered if he would hit me for it, but he just smiled a little and said, "Do that tomorrow, and I think you'll be alright."

When I came home the next day there was no blood on my face and my father was waiting for me. He looked at me and nodded his head and smiled just a little and I smiled back and I'm sure I blushed when he said, "We'll go fishing Saturday, just you and me."

***

My father always kept his word, and so we went fishing next Saturday, the first and last time we ever did something like that. The drive to the ocean was over an hour, and my father said little during the trip. But he hummed to the songs on the radio, and he smiled just a little and winked at me once, so the drive was nice.

We rented a small fishing boat and two fishing rods and bought gas and lunch and live bait and went out past the bay with the engine making a sharp buzzing sound. When he stopped the boat, the land looked miles away and the water was very calm and deep and dark and the boat seemed to dream its way over the sea, and with the engine off the world seemed very quiet. A salty wind blew upon us. My father tossed the anchor into the water and let the line play through his calloused fingers, and I could feel the ocean moving under us and I wondered how deep the water was and what kind of creatures might be swimming underneath our boat right now, and if I were to name our boat what name might I give it. When I dipped my hand into the water it was very cold, and a seagull flew a quick half circle over us and looked into our boat and flew away and its cry sounded like a sad sort of laughter. The seagull seemed beautiful to me, and I thought that I would name our boat *The Gull*.

For bait my father had purchased a bucket of live minnows and I kept the bucket between my feet so that it wouldn't turn over on the trip out to the deep water. I liked watching the minnows play in the bucket; it was like holding innocence between my feet and I wondered if minnows had thoughts and if they ever felt fear. It bothered me that there were so many in the bucket and that we would have to kill them. The ones we didn't use for bait my father said we would freeze for our next fishing trip. If I could have spoken to the minnows, I think I would have hugged the bucket and said, "It's okay; don't worry, it'll be alright," even if it was a lie.

They had given me a bulky orange life jacket to wear but my father had taught me to swim and when he stopped the boat he told me to take it off, it looked uncomfortable. He winked at me and said, "Don't tell you mother," and then he scooped a minnow out of the bucket and pushed a hook into one of its eye sockets and out the other. The minnow twisted and curled when he did that and I thought it horrible to see the minnow wriggling when my father dropped the line into the water. When I asked my father if he thought it hurt the minnow, he paused for a second and said, "No, they don't feel anything."

When both lines were baited and in the water, I watched my father and tried to mimic the way he moved his fishing pole down and up and a grace and a patience I was unused to seeing in him. I wondered if the minnow was still alive on my line, and my father looked happy and he turned to me and said, "Flounder and fluke sound good?"

"Yes," I said, and I think I smiled a little because those names sounded funny to me, *flounder and fluke.* I tugged my line high in the air and there was a sudden rough dancing on the tip of my rod that shuddered my hands and startled me, and my father sounded excited when he said, "*Hey* you got one, Danny, reel him in," and I worked the reel until the muscles of my forearms hurt, my father saying the whole time, "Higher, hold it higher, like *this.*"

I brought the fish to the surface and watched him swim back and forth next to the boat and my father said to lift him out of the water and so I did. The fish still fought very hard and then fell suddenly to the floor of the boat and for a moment we watched him jump and slip and work his gills on the floor and my father said "Fluke. Big one. We'll keep him."

There was a large empty bucket on board for holding fish and my father put the fluke into the bucket and started baiting my line again. My fluke was a big, flat, funny-looking fish with two eyes on the same side of his face which gave him a sad, comical look, and I nearly laughed out loud. The fluke jumped once in the bucket and then lay very still and worked his gills in and out. His eyes were misty and sad, and I wondered if he was looking at me, if he could see clouds, or if before death he could somehow see through time. I wondered what he thought about as he lay there, and I wondered about his heartbeat, and when I touched him he was cold and his skin was very slippery. I said to my father, "He'll die," and my father just said, "That's our dinner in there."

I didn't want the fish to die like that, so I took my father's empty coffee cup and began to scoop seawater into the bucket and over the fish. The fluke's tail curled when he felt the water hit him and my father gave me a funny look when he saw me doing this and he handed me my fishing rod and didn't say anything, so we sat for a while fishing and not talking as I continued to scoop water into the bucket. I could see the disapproval in my father's eyes and the silence was very difficult to bear. Tiny ocean ripples made gentle slapping sounds against the boat's bottom and the cups of water seemed very loud as they entered the bucket. I tried to be quiet about it and hoped that my father didn't notice, and that I wasn't a disappointment. The bucket was soon half full and the fluke began to swim in it, working his gills and his fins and nosing the sides of the bucket and looking for a way to get out.

I didn't want to fish anymore after that but I tried not to show it and perhaps my father noticed and perhaps the ocean noticed because he caught the next fish, and the next, and the next after that. All flukes. Each fish he threw into the bucket and I could hear the fish as they struggled for a moment to find a comfortable place in the bucket and as they tried to find a way out. They were very crowded and I wondered if I made a mistake in filling the bucket, in not letting them die more quickly.

After catching his last fish, my father looked at his watch and said, "Four fish, not bad," so I knew he was ready to leave. He told me to put on my life jacket for the trip back, so I did, and he stood for a moment on the deck of the small boat and looked around and said, "This was a good day," and asked me if I had fun and if I was ready to leave. Before I could answer he walked to the front of the boat and began pulling at the anchor line.

When he was working, he expected others to work also and I knew he would soon find or invent a task for me. I sat in the back of the boat and waited and watched him work. It was a game I sometimes played, watching my father when he didn't know it, trying to catch some glimpse of who he really was. This game was secret and terrible—I knew when I met the true *him* I wouldn't like him very much. And he worked the anchor line into the boat, and I could see the muscles on his back and on his arms stretching and gathering like the strike of a cobra.

My father worked powerfully and rhythmically. The day had grown breezy and cool, with very few boats on the water, and the scents of the ocean were everywhere. One of my feet touched the bucket in a caressing gesture.

The fish had become quite still in the bucket and I wanted to look but I didn't. I feared seeing them dead, or worse, watching them die. And there was a quick sudden splash in the bucket that wetted my face like a baptism, or a great salt tear. I looked into the bucket and the fish were moving very slowly now and their gills were working very slowly and their eyes seemed pained and hazy, and I knew the four big fish had used up the oxygen in the water and that they were suffocating, very slowly and, it seemed to me, with great fortitude. They would soon die, and I looked at my father and silently blamed him for it.

Just then he pulled the anchor from the sea like some great lost treasure, dripping and dirty from the bottom. My father said, "*Aha*," and dunked the anchor into the water over and over to clean off the muck. He spoke over his shoulder and told me he learned this trick from *his* father, and asked me to come up front so that I too could learn it. I didn't answer him, because I had put my face very close to the bucket and hugged the bucket and the fish to my chest and stood up with all of it in my arms.

The bucket was very heavy and my muscles shook with the effort of holding the slooshing water and fish on a tiny boat that now seemed balanced on the tip of a giant's beanstalk. I swayed left and right and I thought for a moment that all would spill, and that would be terrible. The bucket was very cold and very wet against my arms and it was dirty with the slime of a thousand fishing trips. The smell of the fish was very strong, it was a sweet and heavy smell, and the life in them flashed as they felt themselves being lifted and carried, and my face again got wet and my eyes stung with salt. I blinked.

It was difficult balancing, and the bucket was very heavy, and so I set it down on the side of the boat and the boat dipped on that side with this great new weight, and the water inside the bucket grew still. I held the balance of the bucket and I paused a moment and looked at my father's back. The sea and the day too had grown very still and I could hear seagulls playing somewhere; their song was hollow and joyless and seemed thousands of miles away. My father was coiling the anchor line very neatly and was humming under his breath low and sweet. He started to say something to me and then smiled and changed his mind.

I looked from him to the fish and then held the bottom of the bucket very gently between my hands, and with my chin I tipped the bucket into the sea. I watched the fish fall into the sea and when they hit the surface it was like a burst of silver joy and they disappeared very quickly and then were gone.

The sun had grown very red in the sky now and the sound of falling water was loud in the quiet of the dying day and my father said nothing. I felt a coolness trickle my spine as I looked at him. His back was to me but he had stood up very straight and the muscles on his back and neck were taut and his head was turned just a little. He knew. Then he spun about very carefully and looked at me and made sure what I had done.

His walk toward me was careful and very quiet and I wondered what he would do to me. He seemed a giant as he stood over me, and I recall that he placed his hands on my shoulders and gently fumbled the straps of my life jacket. He bent toward me and again I could smell his breath sweet and heavy and I saw a strange flash in his eyes and I thought for a moment that he was going to hug me, but then he slid his hands under my arms and very quickly lifted me from the boat and dropped me into the sea.

I was shocked at the quickness of the thing and the lethal strength in his arms, and the water was much colder than I could have imagined. I was under for less than a second and I thought I would drown, but my life jacket brought me to the surface and I was very cold and began to kick toward the boat very quickly. My father's back was to me and I heard the engine start and, without looking, my father had begun to drive the boat away from me. I swam very hard toward the boat but the life jacket made any sort of real swimming impossible. I screamed for him to wait and for some seconds the front of my trousers went oddly warm in the cold water.

When the boat was small and very far away, I saw it swing a long, lazy circle back toward me, and my father didn't look at me when he said, "Get in." It was very difficult climbing alone into the boat and I hurt my knee badly, but I stayed quiet and shivered as my father drove in and returned the boat and the equipment. I wondered about the fate of the minnows and I thought about tossing them back into the sea, and I knew these were foolish thoughts. He said nothing until we got to the car, and then he looked at me over the roof of the car and he said, "What am I supposed to tell your *mother*, huh? What am I supposed to tell *her*?" And then he said, "Get in," and when he saw my wet clothes, he told me to stop, and then threw a towel at me and told me not to get the seat wet.

On the way back, there was no music and there were no smiles and there was no talking. My teeth had begun to chatter and that seemed very loud in the car so I stopped it and glanced at my father just once. I remember wanting to say to him, "It'll be okay, Dad; everything will be alright," but I said nothing. The day was over and it was getting cold and dark and we drove back home in silence.

***

A few years ago, I workshopped that story with a brilliant author named Melissa Bank. (She wrote a marvelous collection of short stories called *The Girls' Guide to Hunting and Fishing.*) After Melissa and the group discussed my story, Melissa said, "I don't know what else to say. It's just such a successful story." In her comments on it, she wrote, "I can't wait to read your work when it gets published!" At that time, I hadn't yet been published, so I lived off those compliments for several years, and remembered them whenever I felt a little bit discouraged.

This story means a great deal to me. I'm very happy with it, and it's based on something that actually happened to me. But in the real-life version, I didn't throw the fish back into the sea. (And I wish I did.) I think writing this story was my way of revisiting the narrative of my life, and "rewriting" certain things that happened to me. Does that make sense? When a short story is based on you and your life, it's a bit like a personal essay. You get to relive certain moments of your life. But it's *fictional*, and that brings with it a certain silken luxury: *You can rewrite the narrative of your life.* You can fix the mistakes you made, and do the things you wish you'd done.

Please read my story a few times and look for the things that make it a good story. As you read, ask yourself questions: *Who is the bully in the story? Is there more than one bully? Is the ending happy, or sad? Does Danny learn anything? Does he grow?* Also try to spot the *grail, conflict,* and *resolution.* They're all in there, but you have to look for them.

I hope you enjoyed this chapter on writing creatively, and I hope you learned a lot from it. Don't be afraid to read it more than once, because there's a lot of good knowledge in here. I also hope you begin composing your own creative writing. Personal essays and short stories are a great place to start, and that's why I included them here. Writing creatively on your own will help you develop as a writer, and you'll enjoy doing it. Don't wait for your teachers to give you creative assignments, because that might be a very long wait. Go and do them yourself. Talk to your friends, and maybe set up your own writers' group. Have fun with it. Take risks, make spectacular mistakes, and learn from all of them.

And that concludes the final chapter of this book . . . but we're not done yet. I'll meet you in the conclusion. Make sure you read the entire thing. It's a very unusual conclusion, and contains lots of information that will help you in school. And in life.

Conclusion

How to Be a Good Student

When I was in high school, I wasn't a star student, and I should've been. Yes, I was a very good writer, and I was a wizard in my English classes, but I was not a great student *overall*. I was in the *decent-to-good* range. But here's the thing: I could have been a *great* student if I worked harder, was more organized, and got better advice. The only advice I received back then (from adults) was basically this: "Do better, or get punished." That was no help at all, and decreased my motivation to learn. And I didn't know how to fix things.

I remember thinking about my school situation as a teenager, and sometimes feeling a bit sad. I felt that opportunities were passing me by, that I wasn't reaching my full potential, and I didn't know what to do. Do you feel the same way? I'm guessing that many of you do. You are not alone. I know how it feels, and I want to help you, so let's get through this together.

In my first year of college, I was once again a "good" student—not a great one—and again it bothered me. I knew I wasn't living up to my full potential. But that year something very important happened to me. I was accepted into a program to become a commissioned officer in the US Marine Corps. I trained the summer after my college freshman year (I was eighteen years old, and in very good shape), and that experience changed my outlook on life. It changed everything.

BECOMING A GOOD STUDENT STARTS WITH A *DECISION*

When I returned from Officer Candidates School (thirty pounds lighter, with a shaved head and standing a little straighter), I asked myself a simple question, and I remember it like it happened half an hour ago. It was a beautiful September day, and here is the question I asked myself: *If you can make it through Marine Corps basic training, why can't you do better in your schoolwork? If you can complete Officer Candidates School, you should be getting As in your college courses. After all, other people are getting As, and they haven't been through Officer Candidates School. And* you *have.*

It made great sense to me. Right there I made a conscious decision to become a very good student. Did you catch that? Becoming a better student (and a better writer) starts with a *conscious decision* to do it. When I made my decision, I immediately felt better about myself and my life. It was a great sense of relief, and it felt really good. But still, I didn't know what to do. I didn't know how to *change* things. A decision is not enough. Being a good student is an independent skill, and *it must be learned.* Wait, let me say that again: *Being a good student is a skill, and it must be learned.* After you learn it, you have to practice it, and then keep working at it.

In this chapter, I'm going to teach you all my secrets of success, and you won't even have to join the Marines (unless you want to). I want you to become a great writer and a great student. I want you to reach your full potential, and the road to reaching your full potential (and your dreams) starts with *education.* I don't mean to sound "preachy," but I've been around the block a few times, and it's true. It is absolutely true. I don't care what you've done in the past. You're still very young, and you can definitely become successful.

Read this chapter carefully. Read it over and over. Learn and practice the principles I give you. Make a plan, and then stick to your plan. Almost everyone makes a plan of self-improvement at some point (such as diet, exercise, or weight loss). However, when they find out it's not easy, and that success doesn't come in the first two weeks, *they quit.* They go back to their old lives and their old behaviors, which didn't work in the first place. *Don't do this.* Don't give up after two weeks because it's difficult, and because you're tired. The path to success is longer than two weeks. Stick with it. You will get used to your new life, and you will begin to like it, like you're training for a cross-country run. Your body and your mind know when you're treating them well and doing something healthy, and they will reward you with good moods and a feeling of well-being.

After I decided to become a good student—and learned how to do it—and worked at it consistently—my grades improved very quickly. I earned straight As several times in college, and the grades of my last three years of college average out to a 3.9 (with the highest possible score being a 4.0). I became a star student and graduated with honors, and *I want you to do the same.* Please understand this: Becoming a good student is a *skill,* and you must *learn how to do it.* It doesn't come naturally, and it must be *learned.* And one of the most important techniques for scholastic success is to become deeply *organized,* and that's what we're going to talk about now.

It's Time to Get Organized

When I was training in the Marines, I learned a good bit about *organization.* It's valued very highly in the Marine Corps, and it's necessary for success in *any* field. As I discuss organization, I'll be describing my own methods and experiences, because they *work.* I'll keep things simple, and you will learn how to organize your schoolwork and your life, because there is no firm line separating your life from your abilities as a student (or a writer). Here we go.

First, I want you to set up an area in your house or apartment (or wherever you live) to write and study. This should be a good-sized desk with some drawers. If it can't be a desk, it should be a fairly big table, big enough for you to spread out and feel comfortable. If you have your own room, put your desk in your room, so you can shut the door and have some quiet and some privacy.

Try to sit your desk under a ceiling fan, because your school year (at some point) is going to get *hot*. If you don't have a ceiling fan in your room, get a big "box" fan, and point it at your chair. I have both in my home library (which is where I do my writing), and they're a big help when it gets hot. Now, close your eyes and visualize your desk in your room. Picture yourself sitting at it— writing, studying, learning, and thinking. Right now, you may do your schoolwork at the kitchen table, but I don't recommend this.

I know you want to sit in the warm glowing heartbeat of the kitchen and feel connected to your family and to an endless supply of munchies. I get it. However, you will write better (and learn more) in privacy and quiet. So, find a private space in your house or apartment, and set up your writer's corner there. You can go back to the kitchen later.

Now, let's say you have your desk in your room (or some other quiet place). You'll need a computer to sit on top of it. Rather than setting up a desktop computer, I suggest you do your writing on a *laptop* (and make sure you have internet, because you'll need it). I do all my writing on a laptop. In fact, all my books were written on a laptop, including this book you're reading now. I like a laptop because it works very well, and it's portable. You can bring it with you, anywhere you go—school, coffee shop, vacation, your friend's house.

As I write, I put on background noise, either the *wind* or the *rain*, and sometimes the sounds of a summer meadow (I listen to natural sounds and nothing else, courtesy of *YouTube*). These sounds drown out distracting ambient noises, and they help me to concentrate. Do not listen to music (even classical music played low and sweet), because your brain will subconsciously try to follow the musical notes, and you will lose focus and concentration. Make your background noise wind, rain, or nature sounds—and nothing else.

Next, put a *printer* near your writer's desk, because *printing* is the final step in completing a writing assignment (when it's not an electronic submission). When you finish your essay, print it out and bring a hard copy (that means *paper* copy) of your assignment to class, because it makes you look *sharp*. As a former teacher of high school English, I rank student "printer problems" up there with "the dog ate my homework." I have a four-in-one printer in my home library. It prints, copies, scans, and faxes. It's very convenient, was not expensive, and never gives me problems.

Get a desk lamp so you're not working in darkness. The ceiling light will throw shadows on your desk and your work, and that's no good. So, put a cute lamp on your desk, something that makes you smile. If you're a righty, put the lamp on your left. In that position, it will light up your notes when you scribble on paper (and your hand won't block the light). If you're a lefty, put the lamp on your right. I'm a lefty, so if the lamp is on my left, my hand and pencil will cast shadows on the notes I write. It's distracting and annoying, and it hurts my productivity. This is a fine point, but it's very important.

Since I'm a lefty, my desk lamp (an antique brass library lamp with a green glass shade) is on my right. I bought this lamp as a teenager (because I fell in love with it), and it looks great on my desk. The other day, a lady walking her dog near my house gave me a compliment on my desk lamp. Surprisingly, she could see it from the street. It was nice to hear.

After you have your fancy desk lamp, fill your desk with all the scholastic supplies that you will need. When you're writing (or doing homework) and you need a stapler, you don't want to get up from your desk and hunt all over the house for a stapler. It will disturb your concentration and halt your momentum, and you might decide to get a bite to eat, watch some TV, and stop writing or studying for the night. So, what kind of supplies should you get for your writing, your schoolwork, and your beautiful new desk?

Here are the ones that I always kept on (or in) my desk, and still do: Pens and mechanical pencils (sharpening pencils is messy and time-consuming). Notepads with lined paper, and two reams of printer paper. Different color highlighters. A metal stapler and staples (the plastic staplers never seem to work). An accurate clock that hangs on the wall (and doesn't take up desk space). Magic markers (especially black ones) and Scotch tape. A hole puncher that punches three holes. A binder, so you can put your papers in there after you punch holes in them. Also, get another hole puncher that punches a single hole (it's surprisingly useful). A ruler, a big pink eraser, and a few pads of different color sticky-notes. A high-quality pair of scissors, paper clips, and a small trash can near your desk.

But there's one supply to remove from your desk: *your cell phone*. Your phone is a great *distractor*. It will distract you, and it will call you (literally and figuratively). Every time you hear a notification, you will stop writing, look at your phone, and start sending texts. It will destroy your concentration, your focus, and your motivation to learn. Before you start studying, make sure you do the following:

Leave your cell phone in another room.
Leave your cell phone in another room.
Leave your cell phone in another room.

I know this is difficult, but it's very important, and you will get used to it. Remember, your cell phone will be waiting for you after you finish your homework. It's not going anywhere.

Once you acquire your new supplies, you'll need some place to store all your great new stuff. Everything on your desk should have a home. Desk drawers work very well for this, but if you don't have drawers, get some desktop organizers with compartments, and use them to store your pens, pencils and highlighters (etc.). Get your desk extremely neat, organized, and efficient. And now I'm going to say something very important, so listen carefully:

Always keep your desk clean.
Always keep your desk clean.
Always keep your desk clean.

And I mean *perfectly* clean. Whenever you finish your writing or homework for the night, clean your desk so that it looks brand new. Do this *every single day.* Put everything in its place, so that you can find it tomorrow when you do homework. Clean your desk, *every single day.* Once a week, take everything off your desk, take a damp sponge, and wipe your desk down.

There are several reasons to keep your desk sparkling clean. When you come home and sit down to write or study, you don't want to look at a messy desk. It's demoralizing. Also, you don't want a cleaning job *before* you start writing. Instead of having *one* job (writing), you suddenly have *two* jobs: *cleaning* and then *writing.* That's frustrating, and it's enough to push you to your cell phone, the fridge, or the TV. Always make sure you return to a clean desk. Always, always, *always.* You will learn to expect this, and you will grow to love it. It will boost your efficiency, your productivity, and your motivation.

Your desk should always look neat and inviting; make it *call you* to sit down and write and learn. Be aware that your desk "wants" to be messy and cluttered. The flat surface of your desk is a *magnet* that will attract stuff to be placed all over it. That's just the way it is. Don't let it happen, and don't throw stuff all over it, because a messy desk will decrease your motivation to sit and write and study, and it will not make you happy.

And what about all the paperwork you have from all your courses? You have assignment descriptions, old tests you took, papers graded and handed back, worksheets, quizzes, and handouts from your teacher. Lots of stuff. I have noticed that many high school students file all these papers into a single spiral notebook until the notebook holds hundreds of extra pages, is four or five inches thick, and weighs about seventeen pounds. If you do this, *stop doing it*. It's messy and disorganized, it looks terrible, and you'll never find what you're looking for. And now, let's get those papers organized.

Start by getting a good-quality backpack, big enough to hold lots of stuff. Choose one that you like and that does what you need, because you're going to be using it *every day*. Wear it, use it, make it a friend. Get a bright color so you look stylish and cool, but not so bright that it looks dirty after a while. My favorite backpack was red, like a fancy sports car, and it had lots of cool compartments to store lots of stuff. I loved it.

Choose your backpack carefully, and make sure it has pockets so you can organize and carry stuff that you'll need, like pens, pencils, highlighters, and sticky notes. The backpack was always very important to me, and I found it exciting. Think of your backpack as a tiny traveling writer's studio, and make it part of your daily routine.

When you have a backpack, I want you to organize all your schoolwork. *All of it*. Listen carefully now: Every one of your academic classes should have its own folder (you probably won't need a folder for gym). Buy different color folders, and write the name of the class on the outside of the folder (on both sides, in black magic marker). Now, let's say you have a folder labeled "English." Put everything from *English* inside that folder. *Everything*. Handouts. Tests. Quizzes. Papers you wrote.

Even better, organize your papers from back to front, from oldest to newest. Don't throw anything out; it might become important. Put the folders in your backpack, and bring them to school with you *every day*. As soon as you get a handout (or some other paperwork), *put it into its folder immediately*. You will never lose anything, and you will be able to find *everything*. Get the concept? It works.

Folders are a good way to go, but after a while I created my own variation on this method. I bought a box of yellow "clasp envelopes" (ten inches by thirteen inches). Using my scissors, I cut off the top two inches on the *open end* of several envelopes (I cut off the part with the flap and the glue and the metal clasp). In this way, I created "pockets" to store all my schoolwork.

With my black magic marker, I then wrote the names of my classes on both sides of each envelope: *English, Math, Science, History, Philosophy*, etc. I kept them in my backpack, and that's where I stored all my schoolwork. *All of it.* For example, when I received something from my science teacher, I immediately put it into the envelope marked "Science." I like this system more than folders, because these envelopes hold more paper than folders. When an envelope-pocket wore out, I just made another one. I had lots of papers to organize. I could find them all, and I never lost one. *Not one.* I continued to use this system through college and into my doctoral studies as well. For me, it was *perfect*.

And now, I want to talk about something very important. In fact, this is one of the most important elements of your entire plan of organization: the *planner*, sometimes called the *personal organizer*. When I was in college, I was extremely organized. I always knew when I had a test, or homework, or when an assignment was due. And I was never late with anything. *Never.* One thing crucial to my success was a small miracle I discovered called the *planner*. These are planning books that contain a calendar inside, and there are many versions of them. Discovering these was a real breakthrough for me, and I was thrilled. I got a new planner every year, and I lived my entire life through them. There are all different kinds out there, but my favorite was the *academic year* planner.

An academic year planner runs from August to July, rather than January to December (that's called a "calendar year"). I chose my planners carefully, and I always picked a planner with a spiral binding (because they lay flat on the desk). I also made sure it was organized by *week*, rather than month. When I opened my weekly planner on my desk, the left page displayed *Monday, Tuesday, Wednesday*, while the right page displayed *Thursday, Friday*, and the two *weekend* days smushed together. Each day had its own space with lines to write on. It was *awesome*.

Can you picture it? It was amazing how well it worked. I always kept mine in my backpack, and when I got any assignment (including homework), I immediately wrote it in my planner (always in pencil). If something was due in a month or six weeks' time, I wrote that too in my planner. Every day, I looked carefully at my planner, and flipped forward to see the things due next week, or next month, or the month after that. It was a lifesaver for me. It's such a simple concept, but it was incredible how well it worked. And now I want to tell you about another method that works just as well.

Now that I'm a teacher (rather than a college student), I no longer use a book-style planner. I use a big *desk calendar*. It is a marvelous organizational tool and works beautifully. Every June, I buy the academic year desk calendar from a well-known internet store. You'd be surprised how inexpensive they are, and I always choose one with colorful decorations on it (why get something boring?). I also make sure it's the biggest one I can get (twenty-two inches wide by seventeen inches high), because I write notes all over it. My entire life is on that thing, and it's like having my own personal secretary who knows everything and makes sure I miss nothing.

I put the desk calendar on my desk at work (right where it belongs), and there it sits, clear and flat and beautiful. It's the *first thing I look at* when I show up to work every day, and it has never let me down. I love my desk calendar because the entire month is spread out before me in clarity and simplicity. I can see everything at once, and this works for me because I tend to view and understand the world and my life in visual terms. When I *see* things, the universe makes sense to me. And now, let me tell you what I write on my desk calendar.

To put it simply, I write *everything* on that calendar, whether related to school or not. In early September, I take the *school district calendar* and outline the entire school year (and you should too). I write down the first day of school, holidays, days off, open school nights, special events, meetings, ends of terms, reports card due dates, the last day of school, etc. Everything on the *district* calendar goes on *my* calendar.

Next, I put down things in my *personal* life. Birthdays of family and friends, parties, social events. Tickets to shows and concerts. Reservations at restaurants. Phone calls I need to make. Dates to submit books and articles I write for publication. *Am I taking a vacation, or speaking at a conference?* All of that goes on my calendar.

As the school year proceeds, I write down more meetings and events (as they come up), due dates for paperwork, appointments I have, and deadlines for things I need to do. I write down dentist appointments, days I'm bringing in my car for service, and nights I work at my public library. Sometimes, I get an email that tells me about an important meeting taking place in three and a half months. I flip my desk calendar forward, and write down the meeting, the time, and the place. If I don't do that, there is *no way* I will remember that meeting, and I will definitely miss it. Everything, everything, *everything* is on my desk calendar, and I depend on it.

When I write on my desk calendar, I write in a sharp mechanical pencil, and I make sure it's neat and accurate. No rapid scribbling because I'm "too busy." When I make a mistake, I erase it thoroughly and start over. Then I draw an oval around the entry. It looks cool, and it makes each entry clear and easy to read. The entire calendar looks neat and organized. When the month is over, I rip the old month off and throw it out. Suddenly, a new month is before me, full of challenge and beauty and possibility.

And which method should *you* use, the book-style planner, or the desk calendar? They both work extremely well and have their advantages. However, the choice is up to you and your particular organizational style. Think about it. Which do you prefer? Do you want to rely on the book planner that you bring to school every day? Or do you want a big desk calendar on the desk where you do all your studying and writing? You could do both, of course, and have them contain the same information, and this would work very well. However, for a high school student, the *book planner* might work best for you. If you bring it to school, you can write in it as soon as you receive an assignment, and a system like that is very organized and efficient.

Wait, I know what you're thinking: You want to use your *cell phone* as a personal organizer, and that would probably work. In this case, however, I suggest sticking to paper and pencil. Sometimes, you just can't beat the old ways of doing things. Personally, I would *never* put my schedule on my phone. I want to see the entire month spread out before me. Also, sometimes I need a break from technology, and cell phones have been known to get lost. But no matter what method you choose, make sure you choose a system that is clear, simple, and reliable. And then stick to it, and look at your organizer *every day*. In some ways, your life will depend on it.

So, stay organized, and stay on top of your schoolwork, because you can become an excellent student. And now I want to pass along some advice that one of my professors gave me a long time ago, when I was just a little older than you. On the first day of a very difficult college English class, he talked about all the reading we had to do, and he said to the class these exact words: "Don't fall behind, or you might never catch up." And now I'm saying them to you.

I want you to understand those words and remember them, because it's advice I have followed for decades, and it has helped to make me a very successful student. I have six diplomas hanging on the wall in my home library. I can see them right now, and

I'm deeply proud of them. I earned them all *after* high school, so I must be doing something right. And now, I'm passing all my secrets along to you. When a successful person gives you advice about how to become successful, *listen to it*. Yes, I have an aptitude for literature and writing. Other than that, there's nothing special about me. Success is all about consistent hard work over a long period of time. It's a beautiful thing, and it works.

LEARN DEEPLY, AND BEHAVE WELL

And now I want to talk about how you should approach your classes and interact with your teachers. Show up to class well rested, well groomed, well dressed, and well fed. If you're wearing a baseball hat or a hoodie, take it off when you enter the classroom, and don't wait for the teacher to ask you. This gesture shows respect for the teacher and the classroom. High school is very important, and will affect the rest of your life much more than you can imagine.

If you can choose where to sit, always sit toward the front of the classroom (in college, I always sat in the front pretty close to the professor). This makes a very good impression on your teacher. Always pay attention in class, and don't talk to your neighbor. Don't rest your head on the desk, don't make faces at the teacher, and don't yawn. If you *must* yawn, do your best to hide it. Sit up straight, and keep your eyes open and bright. Don't ask to go to the restroom if you don't need to. Don't ask to go as soon as you finish a test. Make no mistake, your teacher sees *everything* in the classroom, and is silently forming opinions of every student in it. You want your teachers to be "in your corner." They will be more inclined to help you.

You already have a reputation among the adults in the building. Every student in your school (including *you*) wears an invisible sign above her or his head. The sign might say, "Nice Kid," or "Hard Worker," or "Very Polite," or "Fun to Have in Class," or "Destined for Success." Or, it might say, "Disruptive in Class," or

"Disrespectful," or "Gives Me a Hard Time," or "Nasty Attitude," or "Troublemaker." What does *your* sign say? Think about it. Try to develop a reputation as a hard worker, a kind person, and a "good kid." At all costs, you must avoid being labeled a "troublemaker." Don't ever be difficult, nasty, or rude to your teachers.

Keep your cell phone out of sight. Better yet, turn it off before class. *Put it away* so that it can't be seen, and *never take it out in class. Never.* Always be prepared for class. A long time ago, when I was a sophomore in college (nineteen years old), I made a friend in one of my classes. He was from India, he was a few years older than I, and he was studying to be a pharmacist. I'll call him *Dev* (this is not his real name). I quickly saw that Dev was brilliant. This was during that time when I was trying to become a good student. I had no one to help me or teach me, and I knew I could learn something from Dev. So, one day after class (we were having coffee in the commons), I asked him a simple question.

"Hey Dev," I said. "I want to get better grades. Can you give me any advice?"

Dev sipped his coffee and nodded. "Here is what I do," he said. "I take good notes during class. Then, after class, I read the notes over. Then, before the next class, I read the notes once again." He looked at me. I saw something deep and bright in his eyes, and I knew he had just told me something very special. *Of course*, I thought. *It's so simple.* I repeated his words to make sure I understood.

"Okay," I nodded. "Take good notes. Read the notes after class. Before the next class, read the notes again."

Dev nodded at me. "If you do this," he said, *"no one can beat you."* Those were his exact words, and I have been hearing them in my mind ever since. Dev had just given me something very precious—and now I'm giving it to *you*. Use it well.

That year, I learned something else from a very good student. I was taking French, and I had become friends with the girl who sat next to me. I'll call her *Chantelle*. Chantelle earned excellent grades, and she was always smiling and friendly. The class was challenging, and our midterm exam was happening in a week. I was a little nervous about it, and Chantelle and I had this brief conversation before class:

ME: So, we've got that test in a week. You think it'll be tough?

CHANTELLE: No, it won't be so bad. I already started studying for it, and it all looks pretty easy.

ME: *What?* You started studying for it? But it's not for a *week*.

CHANTELLE: Well, *yeah* (she shrugged). I always do that. It's much easier that way.

I sat there and thought about what Chantelle just told me. And just like that, my test-taking strategies changed forever. It never occurred to me that a person could study for a test *days* before it happened. Up to this point, I would study for tests the night before, usually from eight to ten at night. Looking back, it's such a silly and ineffective strategy. How could I have missed this? After that brief conversation, I began studying for tests a minimum of *one week* prior to the test. I covered all the material repeatedly (and on different days), and when I sat down for the test, it was as if I had written it myself. Use this method. It works. And now, one more story.

In my junior year of college, I did a study-abroad program to Hungary. (It was amazing. Do this if you can.) I was with a group of students my age, from my university, but there was a guest student with us also. He was a few years older than we, and I'll call him *Cal*. We quickly learned that Cal was from Harvard University, and that he was studying to be a medical doctor. We were all a little intimidated by him, but he seemed like a cool guy, so I became friends with him. We hung out together all the time, and did our best to meet all the girls in Eastern Europe.

One day we were studying together for a history exam, and I looked over at Cal. He was going over his notes. He wrote them in his notebook, in blue ink. I noticed that his notes were all very neat; it was as if he had typed them. I needed a closer look, so I stood behind Cal, and looked over his shoulder.

"What?" he mumbled, still studying.

"Nothing," I said. "I just wanna see what you wrote."

"Mmm," he said, and kept studying.

And there it was. I saw it all. Right there, I learned how to take notes from a medical student at Harvard University. The notes were immaculate. Neat, organized, categorized. There were very few errors, but here's the best part: *They were all in outline format.* When a new topic was introduced, Cal would write the new topic and *underline* it. Then he would write bullet points of related knowledge underneath the topic, and draw a blue *dot* next to each new bit of information. Four or five bullet points for each topic. *Wow,* I thought. *Notes in outline format.* I immediately began using Cal's method, with one slight change: Instead of dots, I used *numbers* like a true outline format. I felt it was a bit more organized.

So, those are three stories about how I learned to become a student. Learn the tips I'm giving you here, and practice them as you grow into your new role. Do all your homework, and bring all the books and materials you need to every class. Make sure you have a notebook for each class, and write notes in it. Keep the notes neat and organized, and always date your notes so you know when you took them. Start studying for a test a week before it takes place. Always bring *two* pens to class, in case one of them runs out of ink (I *always* did this).

Don't be late for class, and don't *cut* class, ever. When you enter a classroom, smile at the teacher and greet her or him. "Good morning, Mrs. Stevens." Or, "Hi, Mr. Davis, how are you?" Your teacher will appreciate this and will quickly form a high opinion of you. I really like it when students greet me as they walk into my classroom and seem happy to be there. Raise your hand at least once during each class to ask or answer a question. Raising your hand *three* times is even better. Always be polite and respectful to your teachers (whether in public or private), because they earned that. You don't have to *like* your teachers, but you must be *respectful* to them. Now, listen carefully:

Never give a teacher an "attitude."
Never give a teacher an "attitude."
Never give a teacher an "attitude."

It's *always* the wrong thing to do, and it will lower their opinion of you. *Immediately.* Every time that teacher sees you, he will see a sign over your head that says, "Nasty Attitude." And there is *nothing* you can do to remove that sign. There are always positive and respectful ways to interact with teachers. If you see students being nasty and disrespectful to their teachers (and I have seen it *all*), *don't follow their example. Don't do it. It's always the wrong thing to do.*

If another student makes a nasty, disrespectful joke about a teacher, *don't laugh* or you become part of that transaction. But here's the good news: *Not laughing* should be easy, because *nasty, disrespectful jokes are not funny.* Think about it: What if someone made a hurtful joke about you in public, and everybody around you laughed. How would *you* feel?

Keep in mind that teachers are human beings. Yes, they can make mistakes and be wrong about things, but you need to be careful about how you interact with them. You are a *student*; they are *teachers.* If you disagree with a teacher (perhaps on a grade you received), you can advocate for yourself politely and respectfully without being confrontational, rude, or disrespectful. You will get much better results that way, and you won't burn your relationship with the teacher.

School is a hierarchical environment, and you are not at the top of the hierarchy. I know that can be frustrating, but it's a *fact,* not an opinion. So, you must learn how to successfully navigate the hierarchy and grow within it. A college is a hierarchy, and so is a workplace, and you'll be in those soon enough. And the rules apply there also.

During a class, you might politely question something the teacher says (perhaps to clarify a point), but don't *argue* with the teacher, don't contradict the teacher (especially in public), don't be confrontational with the teacher, don't make silly jokes, don't cause any kind of a "scene," and don't "hijack" a class by belaboring a point. If you really don't understand something, you can go up to the teacher after class and politely ask for clarification. It makes you look inquisitive, and teachers appreciate this.

Try to show some enthusiasm in your classes, and don't be afraid to smile. Your teachers appreciate this very much. They have devoted years of study to their field, and they enjoy meeting others who appreciate their subject and their class. Try hard to do this, because there are interesting things to be found in every subject, in every classroom, in every teacher. Please understand that *your presence* in the classroom affects the weather in there (more than you think). Every classroom contains an atmosphere, and every-one in there can feel it. Are you having a positive impact on the atmosphere? One way to improve a class is to raise your hand to politely ask or answer a question. It's simple.

In high school, many students don't raise their hand. As a former high school teacher, it was always difficult when I asked a question about the material being studied, and not a single hand went up. *Crickets.* It was very bad for the atmosphere in the room. In those cases, I called on students by name, but I would have greatly preferred a student giving me a voluntary response, rather than having to extract it from an unwilling student. That's no fun, and I always liked having fun in my classrooms. If I'm having fun, the students are having fun also. If the atmosphere feels flat in the classroom, ask yourself what *you* are doing to make things livelier.

Okay, let's pause for a moment and see where we are. You have a place to write and study, you are getting organized, and you are learning how to act in your classrooms and how to interact with your teachers. I have given you some techniques about writing and studying, and now you have the framework for success. How and when do you study and do your writing? How much should you study? *What do you do?*

You have to get engaged with your schoolwork, learn what works for you, and create a routine. I remember starting my doctorate. I wasn't used to sitting and studying for hours every day, and it was very difficult. My body and mind rebelled against it. *No!*, they yelled at me. *Stop! We're not doing this!* I was not used to sitting and concentrating for that long, and in that intensity. It was a shock to my system, and there were days when I wondered, "Will I be able to do this? Can I keep this up?"

Over time, I grew into it, and became very successful at it. I'm not expecting you to do what I did. That was an extreme situation (and personally, I thrive on extremes). But I want you to understand that, by becoming a good student, you are entering a new phase in your life, and you must *grow into it*, and get used to new changes. Your *body and your mind* must grow into becoming a successful student, and you must *believe that you can do it.* The same would be true if you were starting a new diet or exercise program.

In high school, I once ran a half-marathon (thirteen miles). I trained for it, but it was still very difficult. Now, let's take things a step further. Let's say that *you* made it a goal to run a full marathon (twenty-six miles). You cannot start off by running twenty-six miles. Maybe on that first day you jog a half mile, walk a half mile, and go home feeling tired and achy. *Keep doing it*, and don't get discouraged. Stick with it, because you will improve. You will be running five miles before you think it's possible, and bragging about it to all your friends. After a while, your body and mind will start to demand that you run. You will look forward to your morning runs through a forest (hey, it works for me), and you will feel great for the rest of the day.

Keep this in mind as you grow into becoming a good student. It's a path in which hard work and consistency lead to success. Now, what exactly should you do? To begin, I suggest studying *every day*. Yes, study over the weekend also, but remember to have fun and play and spend time with your family and friends. You can do it all.

You will have to create a study routine that works for you. I suggest starting with two hours a day after you come home from school. This is much easier than it sounds. Think about studying for one hour before dinner, and another hour after dinner. An hour at *anything* is an eye-blink. It goes very quickly, but it's a place to start. As a teacher, I sometimes ask our most successful students a very simple question: "How much do you study every day?" And the answer they give me is nearly always the same: "About three or four hours." Does that seem like a lot? It's a fair amount, especially if you play sports after school. But it's also your ticket to success.

When you come home from school, get a snack (I used to have a piece of cake and a cup of coffee), and then start writing or studying immediately. Don't sit and watch TV, or you won't want to get up. TV is hypnotic and puts us into a trance. Go immediately to your writer's corner, and be productive. And now I want to say something very important. When you sit down to study (at your immaculately clean desk), you must *always know what you are going to do*. Set a goal for yourself, and then accomplish the goal. Don't wonder, "What should I work on?" And then hunt through your papers, and flip through your planner, *let's see, let's see . . . ummm . . . maybe . . .* That leads to confusion and indecision. Always know what you need to do, *and then do it*. Know what you need to work on.

Here is my suggestion for you. Start with studying for two hours each day. However, make it your ultimate goal to study *four hours* each day: two hours before dinner, and two hours after dinner. I know that seems impossible right now, but *work up to it*, because *you can do it*. It's not as difficult as it sounds. As you grow into your new role of becoming a student, experiment, try new things, and learn what works for you. Be consistent, be organized, be focused, stick to your routine, and you will eventually become successful. It cannot be otherwise. Don't be discouraged by failure along the way. It's going to happen (I have failed many times), but you must keep working toward your goals.

I am deeply interested in genuine success, and I look to successful people and find great motivation in their success stories. I watch lots of motivational videos on *YouTube*. Very often these people (my role models) are athletes at the top of their field. Sometimes they are Olympic athletes (especially in track and field), and sometimes they are world champions in mixed martial arts (MMA). When I watch an MMA fight, I don't see two people fighting each other. I see world-class skills on display, a lifetime of dreams, and years of hard work.

When people watch an MMA fight, they see a spectacular battle take place for perhaps half an hour. Most people don't see the years of training and sacrifice that led to that meeting in the octagon. *I do.* I see everything. Every time a champion is interviewed, they always say the same thing: *Hard work. Hard work. Hard work.* Hard work led to that meeting in the octagon; hard work is their ticket to success. And then they are handed a gleaming golden belt of a champion, and I can't imagine how that must feel. I would weep with joy. Well, if they can do it, *I can do it* (and so can you). I don't mean I want to become an MMA champion (although that would be quite an honor). No, I want to be at the top of my field, and I have wanted this for years.

When I was in college, I studied six to eight hours a day. When going for my doctorate, I studied twelve to fourteen hours a day, and eventually emerged as the star of the program. Today, I work a full-time job and a part-time job. I get up at three o'clock in the morning to write, and I get to school two hours early every single day. I'm always the first person in the building (except for the custodians, who are amazing). I write again when I get home (if I didn't make my daily goal), and I try to give myself an hour (or two) of relaxation after dinner. *Lather, rinse, repeat.*

Is it difficult? Yes and no. It has become my daily routine, so I have learned to expect it, and it is no longer a shock to my system. It is deeply rewarding to work hard at something, to proceed toward your dreams, and to get results. When one of my books is published and I hold it in my hands, it's like holding an Olympic medal, or the belt of an MMA champion. *I did it,* I say to myself. *I did it!* And kaleidoscopic joy explodes throughout my being.

Again, there's nothing special about me. All my success is the product of lifelong dreams and hard work to make them come true. And it is worth it a thousand times over. When a dream comes true, it is a surreal experience; it is beyond belief. It is a joy that far exceeds words. In this book, I shared my secrets with you, because I want *you* to have that feeling too. *You can do it.*

YOUR CASTLE, YOUR DRAGON, AND YOUR GRAIL

So, you are nearly finished reading this book, and that's quite an accomplishment. But this doesn't mean our journey together has to end. Because you are reading this book, I consider you my student, so I want you to revisit this book often, and learn and absorb the lessons and principles I put into it. And I want you to *keep writing*—not just for school, but for *yourself* and for your future.

So, shut the door to your room, sit down at your desk, and write creatively for yourself—even if no one else ever sees it. Write a hundred private pages. See where it takes you, and see how much you improve as a writer. And what kind of writing can you do for yourself? You can start by doing the two types of writing we discussed in chapter 6: the *personal essay* and the *short story.* These are a great way to start your journey. Writing is the best way to get to know yourself, and to understand your life and the things that are happening (and happened) to you.

Above all, I want you to learn and to grow as a writer, a student, and a human being. And never stop learning. I'm still thrilled with reading and writing and learning, and my hands still tremble when I open a new book. I feel the weight of it in my hands, and smell the ink and the paper, and I wonder about the things I will find there and the beauties I will encounter. I'm about to live inside the mind of a genius for a while and look at the world from a whole new perspective. *What will I see there? What will I find?*

In most cases of being human on planet earth, your journey toward reaching your full potential and living a meaningful life begins with *education*. That's a wonderful thing. I hope your journey through *education* continues throughout your entire life. It will help you to navigate the unexpected detours and obstacles and beauty that come with proceeding down the glorious and glimmering path of being alive on earth and growing toward your dreams.

Before we go, think back to the three parts of a story: the *grail, conflict,* and *resolution.* Your own life is a story, and it contains those three parts. How will you write the story of your life? Only *you* can answer that question, but think of it like this: Your life is a magnificent castle. Inside this castle is a grail—a cup containing your dreams. But there is one slight problem: A fierce and fiery dragon is guarding your grail and standing between you and your dreams. And now I want to ask you an important question: *What is your dragon?*

Is your dragon a lack of confidence? Is it a list of past failures whispering to you that you're "not good enough"? Is it *other people* telling you that "you can't do it"? Is it a secret feeling that you don't "deserve" to achieve your dreams? Only *you* can answer these questions. But I can say this with great confidence: *You deserve your dreams, and you deserve to be happy. You can do it,* but it won't be easy.

And now, I'm going to hand you the keys to your castle. They are shining and golden, and there are *four* of them. Here they are:

1. Hold your dreams in the beauty of your beating heart, and never let go of them.

2. *Believe in yourself*—no matter what happens, and no matter what others say.

3. Work harder than you ever thought possible (with time, you will grow into this).

4. Don't ever give up. No matter what happens, keep going and *don't quit.*

If you use all four keys, you will enter the castle and slay your dragon (and any other frowning dragons that might be lurking there). When you slay your dragons, I want you to step over their lifeless bodies with your head held high, laugh at them, and confidently claim your grail and your dreams. *You deserve it.* You deserve success and happiness. And, when you look inside your glorious grail, what will you find? Inside your grail you will find your dreams nestled among the pages of your vast unwritten future.

And here is your final writing assignment from me: *Go and write your story,* and adore each day of your journey. Compose a future shining with joy, flowered with beauty, and created from dazzling dreams. The due date is up to you.

Resources That Will Help You Learn to Write

A Dozen YA Books That You Will Absolutely *Love*

The Black Stallion, by Walter Farley

Brown Girl Dreaming, by Jacqueline Woodson

The Crossover, by Kwame Alexander

El Deafo, by Cece Bell

Ender's Game, by Orson Scott Card

Fahrenheit 451, by Ray Bradbury

The Illustrated Man, by Ray Bradbury

The Martian Chronicles, by Ray Bradbury

1984, by George Orwell

The Phantom Tollbooth, by Norton Juster

The Poet X, by Elizabeth Acevedo

A Wrinkle in Time, by Madeleine L'Engle

Five Writer's Guides That Will Help You Learn to Write (and Make You Smile)

The Elements of Style, by William Strunk and E. B. White

On Writing: A Memoir of the Craft, by Stephen King

On Writing Well: The Classic Guide to Writing Nonfiction, by William Zinsser

Writing and Growing: Transforming High School Students into Writers, by Timothy Horan

The Writing Life, by Annie Dillard

Seven Terrific Websites for Young Writers

Book Creator: bookcreator.com

NaNoWriMo Young Writers Program: https://ywp
.nanowrimo.org/

NoodleTools: noodletools.com

Purdue University OWL (Online Writing Lab) for Grades 7–12: owl.purdue.edu/owl/teacher_and_tutor_resources/
writing_instructors/grades_7_12_instructors_and_students/
index.html

Teen Ink: https://www.teenink.com/about

Your Public Library's Online Resources

Your School Library's Online Resources

Ten Movies about Writing and Writers (and Sometimes High School)

Dead Poets Society

Finding Forrester

Finding Neverland

Freedom Writers

Last Call

The Man Who Invented Christmas

Midnight in Paris

Misery (This movie is *Rated R*, so watch it when you're seventeen or older.)

Shakespeare in Love (also *Rated R*)

Stand By Me

FIVE YOUTUBE VIDEOS ABOUT WRITING, TRYING HARD, AND BEING HUMAN

"11 Writers: Advice to the Young." https://www.youtube.com/watch?v=q_mlM8M00mw

"John Updike: Advice to Young Writers." https://www.youtube.com/watch?v=s-G5bH7axag

"NEA Big Read: Meet Ray Bradbury." https://www.youtube.com/watch?v=Pqp38_uS-eg

"Never, Ever Give Up. Arthur's Inspirational Transformation!" https://www.youtube.com/watch?v=qX9FSZJu448 (Watch this video whenever you feel discouraged. Trust me.)

"Writing Advice from Neil Gaiman." https://www.youtube.com/watch?v=qg0_FinB6EE

BIBLIOGRAPHY

Annabelle. Email interview by the author. New York. August 15, 2022.

Author William Landay. "John Updike: Advice to Young Writers." *YouTube*, 1:52. March 24, 2013. https://www.youtube.com/watch?v=s-G5bH7axag.

Azat Yolcu. "Why Are We Here? The Story of Man's Continuing Quest to Understand His World (1999)." *YouTube*, 55:15. August 16, 2016. https://www.youtube.com/watch?v=nckoCumq3To [interview with Daniel Boorstin].

Bank, Melissa. *The Girls' Guide to Hunting and Fishing*. New York: Penguin Books, 2000.

Birgitta. Email interview by the author. New York. August 19, 2022.

Boorstin, Daniel. *The Creators*. New York: Random House, 1992.

Bradbury, Ray. *Fahrenheit 451*. New York: Simon & Schuster, 2003.

Bradbury, Ray. *The Illustrated Man*. New York: Bantam Books, 1972.

Bradbury, Ray. *The Martian Chronicles*. Toronto: Bantam Books, 1978.

Card, Orson Scott. *Ender's Game*. Revised edition. New York: Tor, 1991.

DDP Yoga. "Never, Ever Give Up. Arthur's Inspirational Transformation!" *YouTube*, 4:54. April 30, 2012. https://www.youtube.com/watch?v=qX9FSZJu448.

Dead Poets Society, directed by Peter Weir. Touchstone Pictures, 1989.

Dillard, Annie. *The Writing Life*. New York: Harper & Row, 1989.

Elizabeth. Email interview by the author. New York. August 23, 2022.

Emily. Email interview by the author. New York. August 27, 2022.

Farley, Walter. *The Black Stallion*. Illustrated by Keith Ward. New York: Random House, 2012.

Finding Forrester, directed by Gus Van Sant. Columbia Pictures, 2000.

Finding Neverland, directed by Marc Forster. FilmColony, 2004.

Freedom Writers, directed by Richard LaGravenese. MTV Films and Jersey Films, 2007.

Horan, Timothy. *Let's Create Writers: Writing Lessons for Grades Seven and Eight*. Lanham, MD: Rowman & Littlefield, 2021.

Horan, Timothy. *Writing and Growing: Transforming High School Students into Writers*. Lanham, MD: Rowman & Littlefield, 2022.

Jack. Email interview by the author. New York. September 4, 2022.

Jenny. Email interview by the author. New York. September 9, 2022.

Juster, Norton. *The Phantom Tollbooth*. Illustrated by Jules Feiffer. Boston: Houghton Mifflin, 2004.

King, Stephen. *On Writing: A Memoir of the Craft*. New York: Scribner, 2000.

Lamott, Anne. *Bird by Bird: Some Instructions on Writing and Life*. New York: Pantheon Books, 1994.

L'Amour, Louis. *Education of a Wandering Man*. New York: Bantam, 1990.

Last Call, directed by Henry Bromell. Showtime Networks, 2002.

L'Engle, Madeleine. *A Wrinkle in Time*. New York: Laurel-Leaf Books, 2005.

Library of Congress. "Daniel J. Boorstin (1914–2004), 12th Librarian of Congress 1975–1987." Library of Congress, Accessed November 15, 2022. https://www.loc.gov/item/n79065337/daniel-j-boorstin-1914-2004/.

Louisiana Channel. "11 Writers: Advice to the Young." *YouTube*, 11:22. February 1, 2016. https://www.youtube.com/watch?v=q_mlM8M00mw.

The Man Who Invented Christmas, directed by Bharat Nalluri. Parallel Films and Rhombus Media, 2017.

MasterClass. "Writing Advice from Neil Gaiman. *YouTube*, 5:48. July 19, 2019. https://www.youtube.com/watch?v=qg0_FinB6EE.

Meghan. Email interview by the author. New York. September 14, 2022.

Midnight in Paris, directed by Woody Allen. Gravier Productions; Mediapro; Televisió de Catalunya; and Versátil Cinema, 2011.

Miller, Arthur. *The Crucible*. New York: Penguin Books, 1996.

Misery, directed by Rob Reiner. Castle Rock Entertainment and Nelson Entertainment, 1990.

National Endowment for the Arts. "NEA Big Read: Meet Ray Bradbury." *YouTube*, 22:18. October 3, 2017, https://www.youtube.com/watch?v=Pqp38_uS-eg.

Orwell, George. *1984*. San Diego: Harcourt Brace Jovanovich, 1984.

Shakespeare in Love. Directed by John Madden. The Bedford Falls Company, 1998.

Stand by Me, directed by Rob Reiner. Act III Productions, 1986.

Strunk, William, and E. B. White. *The Elements of Style*. New York: Penguin Press, 2005.

Swift, Jonathan. "A Modest Proposal." *Owl Eyes*. Last modified 2022. Accessed October 30, 2022. https://www.owleyes.org/text/modest-proposal.

"Writer's Toolbox." *Gotham Writers*. Last modified 2022. Accessed October 30, 2022. https://www.writingclasses.com/toolbox/author-q-a/camille-minichino?page=9.

Zinsser, William. *On Writing Well: The Classic Guide to Writing Nonfiction*. 30th ed. New York: HarperCollins, 2006.

Index

academic argument essay: challenges with, 7, 8, 98; choosing a side for, 100; climate change assignment example of, 79, 85, 99, 101; conclusion of, 102, 108, 110; controversial issues and, 99; counterarguments part of, 102, 106–8, 109–10; definition of, 79, 98–99; definition of terms portion of, 102–3, 109; essential question, 79; evidence section of, 102, 103–6, 109–10; formal tone for, 114, 120–21; informative essay relation to, 128; ingredients and structure, 101–2; introduction paragraph, 102, 109; outline for, 101–2, 109–10; pride with, 71; prompts for, 99–100; research for, 71, 72–73; summary and commentary in, 103–8, 109–10; teachers views and, 99; thesis statements for, 100–101, 102, 109; title for, 109; topic example, 94; topic sentence example for, 95; video game violence assignment example of, 99, 100–101

academic performance. *See* grades; student, becoming a better

academic writing. *See* scholastic writing

Amazon rainforest assignment example: assignment description for, 128; conclusion for, 130, 143; essential questions for, 79, 84, 129; interpreting quotes in, 138–39; introduction, 130, 140; outline for, 130, 140–43; persuasive approach to, 128; prompt for, 79; research, sources, and citations for, 127, 133–40; subtopics, 129–30, 140–43; thesis statement for, 84,

student, 173–83. *See also* outlines; subtopics
originality. *See* uniqueness and originality
Orwell, George, 32
outlines: for academic argument essay, 101–2, 109–10; for Amazon rainforest assignment example, 130, 140–43; biography assignment example and, 39–40, 50–51, 52–54; conclusion, 55–56; finished, examples, 46–47, 50, 52–53, 109–10, 140–41; five-part, about, 34–36, 93–94, 123; flexibility of, 36, 61, 62–63; focus built into, 59–60; give-and-take relationship with, 57–58, 63; importance of, 35–36, 47, 61, 120, 123; index cards for, 73; introduction, 54–55; for paragraphs, 87, 94–98, 106; personal essay, overview, 148; repeated readings of, 47, 53; research paper, 130, 140–41; rule of three and subtopics in, 36–37, 44–45, 53; short story, 159–60; simplicity, 34; solar system assignment example and, 37–38, 44–47; template, blank, 62–63;

topics and, 34–37, 58–60; World War II assignment example, 38–39, 47–50. *See also* subtopics

paragraphs: audience response to, 89–90; conclusion sentences for, 95–96, 97, 104, 105, 106–8; creating examples illustrating topic sentence of, 95, 97; evidence, 102, 103–6, 109–10; example, 96–97; font for, 92–93; formatting of, 90, 91, 92–93, 97; graduate school experience on writing, 88–89; indenting, 90; length, 91–92, 93, 97; middle section of, 95, 97; plagiarism avoidance in constructing, 88; structure/outline, 87, 94–98, 106; structure replicates essay structure, 94, 97; struggles around beginnings and endings of, 3, 4; summarizing sentence for concluding, 107–8; topic for individual, 94–95, 97
perfectionism, as obstacle, 5, 6
personal essay: beginning with, 192–93; brainstorming questions for, 144–46; conclusion, 148; definition

revising process, 121, 122;
listening to advice role in,
182–83; new perspective
and "taking a risk" in,
123–24, 125; organization
role in, 119, 120, 121, 123;
originality and "taking
a risk" in, 123–24, 125;
personal essay, 71, 72;
poetry, 113; short story,
115; "show, don't tell" advice
in, 118, 119, 123, 124–25;
students on, xviii, 111–25;
"writing to think" and,
112–13, 114
success stories, for
inspiration, 191
surveys, of student writers:
on coping with writing
difficulties, 65–76;
on favorite writing
assignments, 17; process,
1–2; on successes as writer,
xviii, 111–25; on writing
difficulties, xvii–xviii, 1–12
Swift, Jonathan, xii

Talented and Gifted (TAG)
English classes, xii
talking ideas out, 22–25
teachers: advice, listening to,
182–83; asking for help
from, 122, 123; assigning
writing over teaching it, xiii,

xxiii, 31; behavior in class
and with, 183–89; benefits
of learning from different,
15–17, 113, 114; challenges
for, xiv–xv; contradicting
rules and expectations from,
3, 4, 6, 7, 15–16, 77, 112;
creative ideas presented to,
22; curriculum constraints,
18–19; enjoyment taught
by, xxv; freedom in how to
teach, 19; grade discussions
with, 118; as inspiration
sources, 16; plagiarism
response from, 88; respect
and politeness shown to,
186–88; thesis statement
approaches among, 82–83,
112; writing instruction
lacking from, xii–xiv, xxiii,
31–32; writing process
understanding for, xv;
writing prompt creativity
from, 21
tests, preparing for, 185–86
thesaurus use, 66, 67–68
thesis statement: for academic
argument essay, 100–101,
102, 109; for Amazon
rainforest assignment
example, 84, 129, 130,
140; audience relation to,
81; editing process review
of, 86; examples, 84–85,

5–6; embracing, xxv, 121; of ideas, 8, 119–20, 137–38, 140; in research papers, 137–38, 140; success as writer and, 123–24, 125; of writer's voice, xvii, 75

video game violence assignment example, 99, 100–101

vocabulary: diversity of, 68, 69; growth through reading, 69; success with expanded, 113; thesaurus use and, 66, 67–68

voice. *See* formal tone; writer's voice

Wilde, Oscar, xxii

word limit, exceeding, 2–3

words, fixating on: in first draft, 25, 69; ideas focus over, 25, 68, 69; students on, 68; thesaurus use and, 66, 67–68

World War II assignment example, 38–39, 43, 47–50, 59

A Wrinkle in Time (L'Engle), 29

writer's block, xxii, 67

writer's voice: about, xvi–xvii; audience relation to, xvii; developing unique, xvii, 75; editing excessively impacting, 5–6; for personal essay, 147; speaking voice approach to, 24–25, 147; thesaurus use impacting, 66, 67–68. *See also* formal tone

writing, difficulties of: with academic argument essays, 7, 8, 98; with brevity, 2, 3–4, 10; college and graduate students, xviii–xx; confidence and, 4, 5; creativity lacking and, 115; dissertations and, xix–xx; "do it anyway" in face of, xxii; in editing process, 5–6; idea generation for fiction and, 5; overcomplicating ideas and, 115, 116; overplanning and, 70; rambling and going off subject and, 2, 3–4, 121; research papers, 9; under rubrics and rules, 3, 4, 5, 8–9, 10; sentence length, 115; similar experiences help overcoming, xviii; students on coping with, 65–76; students on experience of, xvii–xviii, 1–12; teachers rules differences role in, 3, 4, 6, 7, 15–16, 77, 112; thesaurus use and, 66; time

About the Author

Dr. **Timothy Horan** (BA, MA, MS, MS, DA) has been a commissioned officer in the United States Marine Corps, is the inventor of the School Library Writing Center, and is widely published in the fields of teaching and writing. He has taught literature and writing at the university level, has been the supervisor of a university writing center, has been the editor of an academic journal, and has over twenty years of experience teaching writing, literature, and library science. He has written over twenty-five scholarly articles. This is his fifth scholarly book.